Beyond the Broken Heart

BEYOND THE BROKEN HEART

Daily Devotions for Your Grief Journey

Julie Yarbrough

ABINGDON PRESS
Nashville

BEYOND THE BROKEN HEART:
DAILY DEVOTIONS FOR YOUR GRIEF JOURNEY
Copyright © 2012 by Julie Yarbrough
All rights reserved.

Scripture quotations marked NRSV are from the New Revised Standard Version of the Bible, copyright 1989, Division of Christian Education of the National Council of the Churches of Christ in the United States of America. Used by permission. All rights reserved.

Scripture quotations marked CEB are from the Common English Bible. Copyright © 2011 by the Common English Bible. All rights reserved. Used by permission. www.CommonEnglishBible.com.

Scripture quotations marked ESV are from The Holy Bible, English Standard Version®, copyright © 2001 by Crossway, a publishing ministry of Good News Publishers. Used by permission. All rights reserved.

Scripture quotations marked JBP are from *The New Testament in Modern English* © J. B. Phillips 1958, 1960, 1972. © MacMillan Publishing Company.

Scripture quotations marked KJV are from the authorized (King James) version. Rights in the Authorized Version in the United Kingdom are vested in the Crown. Reproduced by permission of the Crown's patentee, Cambridge University Press.

Scripture quotations marked NASB are from the *New American Standard Bible®*. Copyright © 1960, 1962, 1963, 1968, 1971, 1973, 1975, 1977, 1995 by The Lockman Foundation. Used by permission. (www.Lockman.org)

Scripture quotations marked NIV are from the Holy Bible, New International Version®. Copyright © 1973, 1978, 1984, 2011 by Biblica, Inc.™ All rights reserved worldwide. www.zondervan.com. The "NIV" and "New International Version" are trademarks registered in the United States Patent and Trademark Office by Biblica, Inc. ™

Scripture quotations marked NKJV are taken from the New King James Version®. Copyright © 1982 by Thomas Nelson, Inc. Used by permission. All rights reserved.

Scripture quotations marked RSV are from the Revised Standard Version of the Bible, copyright 1952 [2nd edition, 1971] by the Division of Christian Education of the National Council of the Churches of Christ in the United States of America. Used by permission. All rights reserved.

Scripture quotations marked *THE MESSAGE* are from *THE MESSAGE*. Copyright © by Eugene H. Peterson 1993, 1994, 1995, 1996, 2000, 2001, 2002. Used by permission of NavPress Publishing Group.

Scripture quotations marked TNIV are from the Holy Bible, Today's New International Version®. Copyright © 2001, 2005 Biblica, Inc. All rights reserved worldwide. Used by permission of Biblica, Inc.

This book is printed on acid-free paper.

Library of Congress Cataloging-in-Publication Data

Yarbrough, Julie, 1948-
  Beyond the broken heart : daily devotions for your grief journey / Julie Yarbrough.
      p. cm.
  ISBN 978-1-4267-4438-9 (alk. paper)
  1. Grief. 2. Grief—Religious aspects.   I. Title.
  BF575.G7Y37 2012
  242'.4—dc23   2011049759

12 13 14 15 16 17 18 19 20 21—10 9 8 7 6 5 4 3 2 1

MANUFACTURED IN THE UNITED STATES OF AMERICA

CONTENTS

PREFACE

The death of one you love is like the death of a part of yourself. Grief is the outpouring of emotion and pain that expresses how you feel because of what has happened in your life. As you grieve, you recognize that your life is shaped forever by your experience of the unalterable circumstance of death for the one you have loved and lost.

We all have a story. "We spend our years as a tale that is told" (Psalm 90:9 KJV). In 2004, my beloved husband, Leighton Farrell, died ninety days after the sudden, unexpected onset of an overwhelmingly terminal disease. He was a United Methodist minister for more than fifty years. He was the great love of my life. When he died, my heart shattered into one million small pieces. For a while, I was certain I would die of a broken heart.

Though my soul survived largely intact, I found myself in frightening, unfamiliar spiritual territory. As I sat alone a few days after Leighton died, I was immobilized by shock as a tidal wave of emotion engulfed my entire being. In that moment I came face to face with the inescapable reality of grief.

There was no other name for the indescribable sense of helplessness and the utter hopelessness that threatened to overwhelm me completely. From deep within I knew that I must go *through* grief—that I could not deny it or delay it. I could not wait; I sensed that grief might destroy me if I did not experience it completely.

Like you, I have faced death in the first person. Although I am not a therapist or professional, I have endeavored to fully understand my life-altering encounter with death and grief. Over many months I worked at grief. I read about grief and strained to understand grief. Its compelling urgency became my relentless companion.

As I grieved, many would-be comforters tried to encourage my faith with bereavement platitudes. Unintentionally their empty words hurt me more than they helped me. What I came to understand is that grief is not a crisis of faith; it is a matter of faith. In fact, the long journey through the valley of the shadow of death is the most arduous walk of faith imaginable. Grieving is really a demonstration of faith when you trust God to hold you at your most vulnerable at the time when your life is in pieces and your strength is gone. "The eternal God is your refuge, and underneath are the everlasting arms" (Deuteronomy 33:27 NIV).

Leighton inspired my heart. His life changed mine forever. There is not a corner of my soul that does not bear the everlasting, eternal imprint of his spirit.

On the last occasion that he was in the pulpit, he offered this pastoral prayer, a benediction to my own journey through grief: "We have come this far by faith, and we will continue to walk with our hand in yours wherever you lead us." In life, in death, in life beyond death, God is with you. You are not alone.

Julie Yarbrough
Dallas, Texas

INTRODUCTION

No one really ever expects to grieve. It is not something for which you prepare in life. You cannot anticipate grief or know in advance exactly how you will react when death affects your life, because grief is a real-time experience. Grief never leaves you where it finds you. It may leave you disillusioned or more profound. It may leave you fearful or more confident in the faithfulness of God, depending on how intently you listen to what grief has to say to you.

You may ask, "Why do I grieve?" In my quest to understand grief, I discovered that we grieve because we love. In fact, the more we love, the greater our grief. The ratio of love to loss depends only on the depth of relationship measured by the quality of love. You might say that we grieve in direct proportion to the depth of our love. Few of us would forego love to avoid the pain of grief. Even in the face of grief we give thanks for having loved so deeply that when death touches our lives, we can do nothing for a while except grieve.

Though universal in its fundamental attributes, grief is individual and personal. Just as everyone has a different story, so also everyone grieves differently. I do not grieve in the same way that you grieve, and you do not grieve in the same way that another grieves. This book of meditations on grief and grieving is designed to meet you at your personal place of spiritual need as you grieve. You may want to begin reading the book at the theme or topic that suggests where you are on your journey through grief. You may then want to continue reading forward and, at some time, perhaps review previous months as well. Or you might prefer to pick and choose according to topic; the last section on celebration offers devotions for holidays and special days, which may be read at the appropriate times of the year. Or perhaps you simply will prefer to read from beginning to end. In any case, as you continue reading in the weeks and months ahead, you will sense where you have been and how far you have come on your personal walk through the valley of the shadow of death.

In grief it is often difficult—for a while it may even seem impossible—to focus on more than a single word, thought, or idea when you meditate and pray each day. This is normal. As the mental fog of grief slowly begins to lift, your ability to concentrate will return. It is my experience that spiritual sustenance best nurtures a broken heart when taken in small bites. For this reason, the meditations in this book are intentionally very brief. Over time, the steady diet of care and comfort found in these daily devotions will help to restore your soul until at last you feast again on life.

Because the Bible is, in part, a narrative of human conflict and struggle, and because many of its rich stories illustrate the pain of loss and grief, scripture is a key element throughout the book. Each month begins with a short personal reflection related to the month's theme followed by a *Preparation* scripture and meditation that set the stage for the four weeks to follow. Each week then focuses on a specific topic of grief related to the monthly theme, offering daily meditations that include a Scripture passage, a thought to consider, a prayer, and words of assurance. As a help to your personal meditation, this final takeaway thought is highlighted to help you remember and affirm it throughout the day.

Prayer is one way you express your relationship with God. You may want to adapt the words of prayer included with each day's meditation to the language of your own relationship with God. The prayer ideas are intended to inspire you to personalize your thoughts and expand your heart as you reach out to God in grief.

One meditation each week is devoted to *Rest for Your Soul*. Because grief is hard work, it is important to "put it down" from time to time to rest. Like any faithful companion, grief will wait while you rest. When you return to your grief, it will still be there, though not as insistent as before. Take a day off each week to rest from grief and find rest for your soul.

Each month concludes with a *Perspective* meditation, offering a backward look that summarizes the weekly meditations in the context of the monthly topic. Every month also includes a page for the expression of your personal journey through grief. If you journal, you already know the benefit of having a place to "ex-press," that is, to get out your inmost thoughts and feelings. Perhaps you will want to write about your grief as you meditate through the weeks and months. These pages may be a place to record God's answers to your prayers. Or you may find them a safe, private space for listening intently to your inner voice as it speaks to you in grief.

As you meditate each day on your journey through grief, may the promises of the Bible comfort and encourage you to move from sorrow toward hope— beyond the broken heart.

GRIEF IS SORROW

Did I expect to have the joy without the sorrow? Somewhere in the corner of our shared heart we were aware of the potential for hurt if one of us should die, but we had no idea of the pain of sorrow. Amid my blinding grief and raging sorrow, I encountered my human frailties up close and personal. My spirit vehemently resisted the emotional treachery of loss.

In a sermon on "Grief and Death" my husband, Leighton, said, "I can commend to you a God who loves you, cares about you, who will hold you in his arms if you will let Him." As he spoke, he poured his power and passion into the word cares. He did not know then that his words of grace and comfort would be meant for me.

Preparation

*Be gracious to me, O LORD, for I
am in distress; my eye wastes away from grief,
my soul and body also.
For my life is spent with sorrow,
and my years with sighing;
my strength fails
because of my misery,
and my bones waste away.*
Psalm 31:9-10 NRSV

Thought: Grief is sorrow. When the last guest has left, you find yourself alone with grief. It may be then that the raw sorrow of grief descends upon your broken heart. When one you love dies, sorrow is, in fact, your deep emotional reaction to death—perhaps with painful physical symptoms that mirror your emotional devastation. Your head aches. Your stomach churns. This is how sorrow feels. It is a state of soulless heartache. The sorrow that surrounds death is as real as anything in your life. Yet you are assured that God feels your pain. God shares your tears and sadness. God is equal to your sorrow. God is with you as you struggle in your brokenness. God is with you as you grieve.

Prayer: God, I am broken. Sorrow surrounds me; sorrow is deep within me. You alone know my inmost heart. Amen.

Assurance: **God knows my sorrowing heart.**

Week 1 – Shock

Day 1

My soul is weary with sorrow;
strengthen me according to your word.
Psalm 119:28 NIV

Thought: Grief is shock at the interruption of life's plans. Your initial reaction to death is shock. Shock plunges you headlong into sorrow. In grief, shock and sorrow are inextricably linked. In the emotionally arduous hours and days that follow the death of your loved one, you are shocked and stunned by the bitter reality of death. God uses shock to protect you from the rude impact of death. God understands completely what has happened even though you do not. Rely on God's strength.

Prayer: God, I am shocked by the death of my beloved. How can this be my reality? My soul is weary with sorrow. Give me strength, I pray. Amen.

Assurance: **God knows that I am in shock.**

Day 2

The cords of death entangled me,
the anguish of the grave came over me;
I was overcome by distress and sorrow.
Psalm 116:3 NIV

Thought: Shock is a front-end collision with human mortality. On impact, you experience the full force of shock. You simply cannot believe that the one you love has died. Even if you were there at the last breath of your loved one, there is utter disbelief. If death occurred suddenly and unexpectedly, your shock is intensified by the unreality of circumstance and the unfairness of death. It is incomprehensible that your loved one is gone. For a while you may feel strangled as anguish, distress, and sorrow overcome you. God is with you through the shock of grief.

Prayer: God, somewhere in the depth of my mind I am grasping at the reality of death. But the finality of death is still too shocking. I cannot think. Help me in my distress. Amen.

Assurance: **God will untangle my heart and soul as I grieve.**

Day 3

O my Comforter in sorrow,
my heart is faint within me.
Jeremiah 8:18 NIV

Thought: In shock, you feel faint. Even if death was expected, you are out of balance because of what has happened. Death can cause emotional, mental, and even physical shock. You may be unable to hear what others say to you as they try to explain what happened. When you experience shock, it is not unusual to feel detached and disconnected from yourself and from others. This is full-blown shock. God upholds you when you are faint from shock.

Prayer: God, I am usually so strong and capable. But I am scarcely functioning. Uphold me in body and in spirit. Amen.

Assurance: **When I am in shock, I can yield to the power of God's protection.**

Day 4

How long must I bear pain in my soul,
and have sorrow in my heart all day long?
Psalm 13:2 NRSV

Thought: Shock enshrouds you in its protection, which at once insulates and smothers you. You may go through the rites and rituals of death with vague detachment from the surreal perspective of shock. Perhaps you remember; perhaps it all seems like an out-of-body experience. Yet grief insists that you comprehend the reality of death so that one day you will no longer have sorrow in your heart. God is here. God alone knows your sorrow.

Prayer: God, I am in pain in my soul. It is so great that I can hardly bear it. I am distraught over the death of my beloved. This does not feel like love. Amen.

Assurance: **God understands my pain.**

Day 5

I will turn their mourning into joy,
I will comfort them, and give them gladness for sorrow.
Jeremiah 31:13 NRSV

Thought: When you are in shock, it is difficult to imagine ever again feeling anything. Comfort? You are numb, dumbfounded by death. Gladness? It seems impossible when sorrow overwhelms every fiber of your being. Joy? For now, it is a remembrance of that which has passed away. One day your sorrow will cease and mourning will turn into joy. God comforts you now.

Prayer: God, I feel nothing except my searing sorrow. Are your promises really for me? Help me in this moment so that I may yet live. Amen.

Assurance: **Though it may seem impossible to believe God's promises right now, I know they are true.**

Day 6

The LORD will be your everlasting light,
and your days of sorrow will end.
Isaiah 60:20 NIV

Thought: You listen at the door, expecting your loved one to return, hoping against hope that your dawning reality is only a bad dream, like a nightmare that frightens and then quickly fades. Shock is darkness, a place of emotional blackout. For a while you must grope through the unfamiliar darkness of death. Somewhere there is yet light, even everlasting light. God's light surrounds you amid the darkness of shock and sorrow.

Prayer: God, thank you for the assurance of light. Through the darkness of my sorrow, shine your light into the corners of my broken heart. Amen.

Assurance:. **God is my everlasting light.**

Day 7 – Rest for Your Soul

*The LORD has added sorrow to my pain; I am worn out with
groaning and find no rest.*
Jeremiah 45:3 NIV

Thought: When shock has taken up residence in your heart, your sustained pain and sorrow are emotionally and physically wearying. You may not be able to sleep, or your sleep may be restless and wakeful. Your dreams interrupt you with hope and then quickly remind you of death. Your mind cannot turn off. You find no rest for your body or soul. You must do nothing for a while to recover physically from the shock of grief. Begin today. Remember to breathe. Consciously inhale. Consciously exhale. Step outside for fresh air. Breathe. Rest. There is life beyond grief.

Prayer: God, my exterior is stalwart, but I am worn out with my inward groaning. There is no rest for my body or soul. But I know that there is rest in you, who gives life. Help me to rest, to breathe, to live. Amen.

Assurance: **God wants me to care for myself even in my sorrow and pain.**

Week 2 – Anger

Day 1

Be angry but do not sin.
Ephesians 4:26 NRSV

Thought: Grief is anger at the untimeliness of death. When shock gradually lifts, anger may show up unannounced. Anger may surprise you with its force and power. You are not prepared for its full frontal assault on your heart. Anger thrives and consumes vital energy if you provide a place in your heart for it to take root and grow. Anger is a manageable, short-term reaction to the death of your loved one.

Prayer: God, I am shocked by the anger in my heart. I want to lash out and blame someone for the death of my loved one. May my anger not become sin. Amen.

Assurance: **Anger is a normal response to the injustice of death.**

Day 2

Do not be quick to anger.
Ecclesiastes 7:9 NRSV

Thought: Anger is a common emotional reflex to your separation from the one loved and lost to death. Yet anger is an emotion you are expected to ignore and resolve, especially when you grieve. Because society sees anger as a sign of weakness, you may feel pressure to repress your anger. When you deny your anger, you may experience both physical and emotional symptoms that add to your pain of loss. When you acknowledge your anger, then you are ready to work toward its positive resolution.

Prayer: God, I am usually not an angry person. Yet I am so angry in my heart right now that my loved one died and left me. Help me to understand this anger that separates me from you. Amen.

Assurance: **Anger is a by-product of grief.**

Day 3

Put aside all bitterness, losing your temper, anger, shouting,
and slander, along with every other evil.
Ephesians 4:31 CEB

Thought: It is hard work to sort through your emotions after death. As you confront anger, you realize that it is not wrong to experience it as long as you understand its cause and manage it constructively. Think about the target of your anger. Is it your husband or wife, your mother or father, or other family members? Are you angry at doctors or medical personnel who could not save your loved one? Are you angry at friends who do not understand your grief? Are you angry at yourself? Are you angry at God? Be honest with yourself about your anger.

Prayer: God, I am angry that there was no happy ending to life. And I confess that I am angry that you did not intervene to spare the life of my beloved. Help me to put aside my anger. Amen.

Assurance: **Instead of nurturing anger, I can name it and confront it.**

Day 4

Let everyone be quick to listen, slow to speak, slow to anger; for your
anger does not produce God's righteousness.
James 1:19-20 NRSV

Thought: When anger occupies your thoughts, it reminds you of your guilt and regrets. Most survivors have some regret or guilt, whether real or imagined. Perhaps your anger is driven by the futility of what "might have been." Or you may have guilt and regret about the "could, would, and should" of grief. Listen to what your heart is telling you about your anger.

Prayer: God, my mind is infested with anger. My guilt and regret occupy precious space in my mind and heart that I need for grieving. May I be slow to speak and slow to anger but quick to listen to you. Amen.

Assurance: **When I identify my unresolved issues of guilt and regret, I am able to release them.**

Day 5

Love does not dishonor others, it is not self-seeking, it is not easily angered, it keeps no record of wrongs.
1 Corinthians 13:5 NIV

Thought: Love is not easily angered. Grief may cause unfamiliar anger to surge in a momentary lapse of love. Slowly you resolve your anger by giving it latitude and allowing it to abate over time. You abandon anger when you realize that it really has no part in love.

Prayer: God, I feel the effects of anger on my body and soul. I pray for the resolve to let it go in the name of love. Amen.

Assurance: **It is easier to release anger than to hold on to it.**

Day 6

Refrain from anger, and forsake wrath!
Psalm 37:8 ESV

Thought: Sometimes in grief you simply must be angry for a while until you get it out, examine it, and understand it. Although anger is unhealthy if it escalates beyond reason or is expressed in harmful ways, for some anger is a necessary part of grief. If this is your experience, at some point likely you will realize that you are unwilling to spend more of your mental resources on the nonproductive emotion of anger. You overpower your anger when you forgive. Determine whom or what it is you need to forgive.

Prayer: God, I do not want to be angry forever. May I recognize the need to forgive, even as you forgive me for my anger in grief. Amen.

Assurance: **I feel immediate relief when I forsake anger.**

Day 7 – Rest for Your Soul

Do not let the sun go down on your anger.
Ephesians 4:26b NASB

Thought: It is exhausting to be angry all the time. Anger consumes your mind and frays your spirit. Even if you let it go and forgive, anger may still flare up from time to time along your grief journey. It is difficult to forget the indignity of death. Resolving your anger before the sun sets each day is a habit worth acquiring. When there is no carryover of anger from day to day, you experience the benefit of release.

Prayer: God, I need to put down my anger and rest today. Help me resolve each day to master the anger of grief. Amen.

Assurance: **I let go of my anger a little more each day.**

Week 3 – Fear

Day 1

Out of my distress I called on the LORD;
the LORD answered me and set me free.
With the LORD on my side I do not fear.
What can man do to me?
Psalm 118:5-6 RSV

Thought: Grief is, in part, fear of the unknown, of how life will be without your loved one. Fear is part of the grieving process. In grief you encounter new fears every day. It may seem as if fear cloaks you every minute of every day. Grief magnifies your human capacity for fear. When someone you love dies, what you fear most becomes reality. Though fear is a common response to death, it need not be a permanent fixture in your life.

Prayer: God, I am in distress. Fear has a powerful grip on my heart and mind. I pray that I may feel your presence so that I will not be so fearful every day. Amen.

Assurance: **I will not allow fear to define my life.**

Day 2

For I, the LORD *your God, hold your right hand;*
it is I who say to you, "Do not fear,
I will help you."
Isaiah 41:13 NRSV

Thought: When your world is shaken by the death of your loved one, fear ambushes you when you are unprepared and least able to defend yourself. The power of fear is that it threatens to paralyze you. For no other reason than your grief, you may suddenly feel incompetent. Fear entices you to feel hopeless. You recognize the hold that fear has on your life when your confidence becomes self-doubt and your certainty becomes second-guessing. Fear is overcome by the strength of God's hand.

Prayer: God, I need you to hold my right hand because I am immobilized by fear. May I hear your voice whisper in my heart, "Do not fear." God, help me. Amen.

Assurance: **I have within me the spiritual resources to disable fear.**

Day 3

It is the LORD *who goes before you. He will be with you; he will not*
fail you or forsake you. Do not fear or be dismayed.
Deuteronomy 31:8 NRSV

Thought: In grief, your strength and wisdom are sometimes reduced to weakness by fear. When you are wounded and broken, you are vulnerable to the kaleidoscopic projections of fear. You may fear that you will become ill or that you will get hurt. You may fear that you do not have enough resources. You may fear your own death or that you will die alone. You may fear that you will lose someone else close to you. You may fear the unknown. The list goes on and on. The power of fear is conquered by the power of faith.

Prayer: God, I can do nothing except walk in your steps as you go before me, believing that you will not fail me or forsake me. I am dismayed. Help me conquer my fear. Amen.

Assurance: **When I write about my fear, I put it in perspective.**

Day 4

*For God has not given us a spirit of fear, but of power and of
love and of a sound mind.*
2 Timothy 1:7 NKJV

Thought: Your intensified sense of fear is an effect of grief. Because of the death of your loved one, your life seems unstable. Every new event and issue may challenge your very will to survive. Sometimes it is easier to succumb to fear than to defy it. Yet God has given you the gifts of power, love, and a sound mind.

Prayer: God, you have not given me a spirit of fear, yet I am fearful of so much. Grief tests my sound mind. You alone are power and love. Amen.

Assurance: **I am endowed with power, love, and a sound mind.**

Day 5

*Therefore we will not fear, though the earth should change,
though the mountains shake in the heart of the sea;
though its waters roar and foam,
though the mountains tremble with its tumult.*
Psalm 46:2-3 NRSV

Thought: Grief feels like a catastrophe that is personal and life-changing. The earth changes, mountains shake in the heart of the sea, waters roar and foam, mountains tremble with tumult. Grief is like a tsunami with its lethal undertow of pain and sorrow. You react with fear—agitation, anxiety, disquiet, and apprehension. Where is your safe haven when death upends your life? Your refuge is in God, who never changes.

Prayer: God, you are my refuge and strength. Be present to me at this time of great tumult in my life. It is easier to say that I will not fear than it is to be unafraid. Amen.

Assurance: **I will not fear. God is my very present help in trouble.**

Day 6

*Do not fear, for I am with you,
do not be afraid, for I am your God;
I will strengthen you, I will help you,
I will uphold you with my victorious right hand.*
Isaiah 41:10 NRSV

Thought: When your loved one dies, grief suggests that every other experience in life may have a worst-case outcome. Is this the ordinary fear of doubt and insecurity or the learned conditioning of grief? With the death of your loved one, you may lose the mastery of your emotional equilibrium for a while; but you can respond with courage to God's charge: do not fear, do not be afraid.

Prayer: God, I claim your strength and your help as my own. Uphold me with your victorious right hand until I am at last free of my fears. Amen.

Assurance: **When my fear is defeated, my self-confidence is restored.**

Day 7 – Rest for Your Soul

Be strong and courageous; do not be frightened or dismayed, for the
LORD your God is with you wherever you go.
Joshua 1:9 NRSV

Thought: When you do what you fear, you disable the power of fear. When you deny fear, you become stronger. When you defeat fear, you turn it into courage. At last you realize that you are no longer fearful all the time. Take a well-deserved rest from fear today.

Prayer: God, it is difficult to grieve and be fearful every day. Today I pray for rest from my daily dismay. You are with me wherever I go. I do not need to defend myself today from fear. Amen.

Assurance: **When I live without fear, I am strong and courageous. I will rest today from fear.**

Week 4 – Confusion

Day 1

My body is racked with pain,
pangs seize me…
I am staggered by what I hear,
I am bewildered by what I see.
Isaiah 21:3 NIV

Thought: Grief is confusion. It is the muddle of feelings, questions, and demands that cannot be separated into neat piles. Your body may be racked by real pain, whether emotional or physical. You may be bewildered by the empty chair at the kitchen table. Or you may start to speak to someone who is no longer there. Confusion is going to bed without saying goodnight to the one you love or wandering around a too-large house with painful memories. The confusion of grief slowly melts away as physical and spiritual order are gradually restored.

Prayer: God, I am staggered by what I hear and by what I do not hear. I am confused. This must be grief. You alone know my mixed-up heart. Amen.

Assurance: **My confusion is a normal part of grief.**

Day 2

All were amazed and perplexed, saying to one another,
"What does this mean?"
Acts 2:12 NRSV

Thought: "What does this mean?" "Why did he/she die?" "Why my child?" When your loved one dies, you are tormented by questions. You want answers because you are perplexed. When tragedy strikes, you are stunned. For a while, questions may be the constant theme of your chaotic thoughts. When you ask "Why?" it is a cry of pain that reflects your anguish and confusion. It is the emotional response of your heart to grief.

Prayer: God, can you tell me, "What does this mean?" I am amazed by the power of death. I do not understand. For now, there are no answers except that I am not supposed to know. Amen.

Assurance: **God will reveal to me the extent of the mystery that I need to know.**

Day 3

We are hard pressed on every side, but not crushed...
2 Corinthians 4:8a NIV

Thought: At times in grief you may find that your very will to survive is hard-pressed by the insistence of confusion and chaos. Grief may feel like an oppressive weight that threatens to destroy your will to live. Though you are hard pressed, through the power of faith you are not crushed by grief.

Prayer: God, I feel the weight of my hard-pressed grief. It could easily crush my soul and spirit. May I trust your strength rather than my own. Amen.

Assurance: **I will not be crushed by the chaos and confusion of grief.**

Day 4

...perplexed, but not in despair.
2 Corinthians 4:8b NIV

Thought: You are perplexed by never-to-be answered questions about the death of your loved one. There is mental and emotional confusion about the vast mystery of death. In dark moments you tiptoe to the precipice of grief and peek over the edge into the unknown. You ask, perhaps again and again, "Why did he or she die and not me?" The questions of grief echo. Perplexed, you wait in faith for answers. When you trust that God knows the why, there is no place for despair, even in grief.

Prayer: God, I am perplexed. For me there is no order or sense or reasoning in death. I torture myself to know the unknowable. Penetrate my confusion with your presence. Amen.

Assurance: **Though I am perplexed by death, I wait on God and do not despair.**

Day 5

...calamity overtakes you like a storm
...disaster sweeps over you like a whirlwind
...distress and trouble overwhelm you.
Proverbs 1:27 NIV

Thought: Death feels like a calamity, indeed, the very worst sort of natural disaster. Confusion is at the eye of the storm of death. It is the whirlwind within your mind and spirit. Confusion sweeps into your well-ordered life when distress and trouble overwhelm you. For a while you take cover, hide, and wait for the storm to pass, knowing that the landscape of life is forever altered by death. You weather the storm because God's abiding presence never changes.

Prayer: God, I am overwhelmed by the forces of death and grief. In your mercy, shelter me while I wait for the confusion of grief to pass. Amen.

Assurance: **Storms do not last forever. This storm will pass.**

Day 6

My soul is overwhelmed with sorrow.
Mark 14:34 NIV

Thought: When your soul is overwhelmed with sorrow, it is often impossible to concentrate on the business of this world. Yet you are forced by the demands of death and the needs of your ongoing life to make choices and decisions. Business can easily overwhelm you when your soul is filled with sorrow. When emotional confusion begins to subside, your grief may feel naked and exposed. Yet deep within, yours is an unconquerable soul because it is fortified by the unshakeable love of God.

Prayer: God, even though I am usually able to manage the business of life, I am overwhelmed with sorrow. I hardly recognize my incapacity. Is this the way it will always be because of the death of my beloved? Clear my mind and heart so that I may think and live in your presence. Amen.

Assurance: **Sorrow is not a permanent condition of my soul.**

Day 7 – Rest for Your Soul

The LORD your God is with you,
he is mighty to save.
He will take great delight in you,
he will quiet you with his love.
Zephaniah 3:17 NIV

Thought: God is with you in the confusion of your sorrow. Rely on God's might to save you unto life—your life. God takes delight in you, especially when you entrust your sorrow to God's transformative power. This day put aside confusion. Today you are not overwhelmed or perplexed. Today you are at rest. Expect God to quiet you with unfailing love.

Prayer: God, amid the confusion, whirlwind, and storm in my soul, I need to rest. Refresh me, I pray. Quiet me with your love. Amen.

Assurance: **God knows my inner tumult and quiets me with unfailing love.**

Perspective

Even youths will faint and be weary,
and the young shall fall exhausted;
but those who wait for the LORD shall renew their strength.
Isaiah 40:30 NRSV

Thought: A symptom of grief that may easily overwhelm you is fatigue—of your mind, heart, body, and soul. It is exhausting to grieve every day. Your strength is consumed by your sorrow and endless tears. God gives you the strength to bear your sorrow. You do not bear it alone.

Prayer: God, I am exhausted by the daily sorrow of my grief. When will my strength be renewed? I am waiting for you. Amen.

Assurance: **If I wait on God, my strength will be renewed.**

Grief Is Sorrow

_____

_____

_____

_____

_____

_____

_____

_____

_____

_____

_____

_____

_____

_____

GRIEF IS PAIN

The events of public leave-taking—the "re-funerals," as I began to call them—numbered seven when they were finally over after almost one year. Six months after Leighton's funeral, another service was held at the church where he served until he became ill. There had been remembrance moments there immediately after he died, but there was need for a more structured memorial service as well. On that January night, I expected to see him in the sanctuary, standing in the pulpit, wearing his vestments, and surrounded by other clergy. He was not. It felt like another funeral—his absence a visual reminder of the enormity of my loss, which perfectly articulated my grief. It was as if he had died all over again. My pain and sorrow were renewed and refreshed. I had no will to be brave and strong. I was not. Fatigue, numbness, and the shroud of shock—which had been my only allies immediately after Leighton's death—had gone on to serve another with a grief newer than mine.

There followed four smaller yet no less painful services and ceremonies that invoked Leighton's name and remembered his life, ministry, and contribution to others and institutions. My heart broke with each bittersweet moment that honored his memory.

Almost a year after he died, I attended the memorial service at the North Texas Annual Conference. His colleagues were there—clergy friends who knew and loved him and appreciated his leadership in The United Methodist Church. Surviving spouses and family members were invited to process with lighted candles and stand to honor the memory of the deceased as their names were called.

> *Subliminally I braced for the event, for yet another moment of public grief. Despite my resolve, I felt the familiar physical symptoms of grief as they waved through my body. I had underestimated the full force of another public confrontation with reality. My best intentions were gone in an instant as tears sprang forth from the depth of my love for the one remembered and lost to me in death. I was powerless to be anything or anyone other than what I was at that moment—broken, human, and in pain. The message resounded in my head as it pounded in my heart, "He is gone from this earth. He is dead. He is dead."*

Preparation

My anguish, my anguish! I writhe in pain!
Oh, the walls of my heart!
My heart is beating wildly;
I cannot keep silent.
Jeremiah 4:19 NRSV

Thought: Grief is the pain of wanting things to be as they were once, yet knowing that they never will be again. In faith you believe beyond doubt that your loved one is with God, but you are human. You are in pain. You hurt. God gives you strength to endure the desolate pain of grief. God promises that grief and pain will not last forever, that you will be restored and made whole again. God is with you as you grieve.

Prayer: God, I cannot keep silent. Hear my cry of pain. My heart is beating wildly with the anguish of grief. Amen.

Assurance: **In grief, the head cannot lead; it must follow the heart.**

Week 1 – Worry

Day 1

"Do not worry about your life."
Matthew 6:25 NRSV

Thought: Grief is worry. In fact, your most faithful companion in grief may well be worry. Even if you are not someone who chronically or habitually worries, it may surprise you how much of grief is framed in worry, at least for a while. Fear drives and inspires worry when you grieve. Fear and worry are partners in grief.

The emotional pain of grief intensifies worry. When you understand this about grief, you are better able to put worry in perspective. As your fear slowly diminishes, worry will release its hold on your mind and heart.

Prayer: God, you command me not to worry about life. But I am in pain, and worry consumes my mind. May I understand your command even if I am not entirely able to give up all of my worry right now. Amen.

Assurance: **As I overcome fear, my worry subsides.**

Day 2

"Can any of you by worrying add a single hour to your span of life?"
Matthew 6:27 NRSV

Thought: Worry is a non-productive use of your precious mental and emotional resources. Normally your life is probably more about concern than worry—concern for others, concern for daily responsibilities, concern for yourself. In grief, concern easily escalates to worry. Yet worry cannot add a single hour your to life; on the contrary, worry has been proven to shorten life. Worry has no beneficial effect, yet it is a real part of grief. Worry is defeated by persistent trust in the care of God.

Prayer: God, it seems that worry is part of my every thought since the death of my beloved. It is not like me to worry all the time. Still my mind to receive your Spirit. Amen.

Assurance: **God is larger than my worry.**

Day 3

"Do not worry."
Matthew 6:31 NRSV

Thought: Jesus said, "Again the command: Do not worry." Worry is a learned habit, one that is well-taught by grief. Worry is really an acquired state of mind and thought nurtured by grief. As with all habits in life, overcoming worry is mind over matter. When worry is the sole substance of your thinking, say to yourself, "Do not worry." As you intentionally learn to recognize worry, you disarm its power over you as a symptom of grief.

Prayer: God, it is easy to remind myself not to worry, but it is very difficult not to worry. Direct my thoughts away from worry toward you. Amen.

Assurance: **Worry is a side-effect of grief, not a permanent condition.**

Day 4

"Today's trouble is enough for today."
Matthew 6:34 NRSV

Thought: When you grieve, worry is a natural reaction to questions you ask every day, such as "What should I do about . . . ?" and "What will I do when . . . ?" You may worry about your health, your family, or your financial security. When the pain of grief is exacerbated by worry, every concern takes on larger than life importance, meaning, and significance. As you grieve, confront only today's troubles. They are sufficient for today. There is hope for tomorrow.

Prayer: God, today's trouble is indeed enough for today. I am grateful that you give me life for each new day. I know that in you there is relief from today's trouble. Amen.

Assurance: **Worry cannot resolve today's trouble.**

Day 5

"Do not worry about tomorrow . . ."
Matthew 6:34a NRSV

Thought: Anxiety is worry born of grief-driven uncertainty. Anxiety is the product of your projection about tomorrow and what may or may not come to pass. Most often, what you worry about for tomorrow never even happens. Anxiety may be an expression of your fear of the unknown. After the death of your loved one, anxiety may cause unaccustomed distress or panic because of unknown outcomes or long-term possibilities. That is the prospect for tomorrow. This is today. Abandon tomorrow and live only in this day.

Prayer: God, I scarcely live today because I worry incessantly about tomorrow. You alone know. May I release my grip on tomorrow so that I may be present to you today. Amen.

Assurance: **Life becomes more manageable when I do not worry about tomorrow.**

Day 6

". . . for tomorrow will bring worries of its own."
Matthew 6:34b NRSV

Thought: Agonizing is the most extreme form of worry. It is the form of worry that feeds your circular inner monologue, that endless conversation of the mind that asks, "What if . . . ?" You agonize subconsciously when you worry about difficult decisions and seemingly hopeless situations. As surely as the sun rises again, tomorrow will bring worries of its own. Agonizing about tomorrow's worries today is an insidious pitfall of grief. Rather than worrying about "What if?" reframe worry into the possibility of "What now?"

Prayer: God, I struggle with worry every day. I hear myself agonizing about the vast unknown of my life. Teach me the quiet of the mind that is yours. Amen.

Assurance: **I conquer fear and insecurity by resisting needless worry about tomorrow.**

Day 7 – Rest for Your Soul

In peace I will lie down and sleep,
for you alone, LORD,
make me dwell in safety.
Psalm 4:8 NIV

Thought: When worry is the habit of your mind, it is often difficult to lie down or sleep. Worry keeps you from sleep. Worry wakes you from sleep. Worry robs you of sleep. Yet in grief, sleep is your most restorative ally. Sleep ensures that your body can function, even when your mind is overwhelmed by sorrow and pain. Sleep can be either restful or restless. When you lie down to rest your body, give worry a rest as well. This ensures rest for your soul.

Prayer: God, as I worry and grieve, you alone keep me safe—from myself, from today, and from what may lie ahead. May I rest my soul in you this day. Amen.

Assurance: **I entrust my worry to God's safekeeping.**

Week 2 – Loneliness

Day 1

Turn to me and be gracious to me,
for I am lonely and afflicted.
Psalm 25:16 NRSV

Thought: Grief is loneliness. Grief is the emptiness of aloneness. The impassioned cry of the psalmist to God was offered from the same place of personal loneliness and isolation that you experience in grief. Isolation is the feeling of being bottled up and locked away from life. The psalmist acknowledged loneliness and called it an affliction. In grief you experience loneliness as pain. For a while, you are afflicted. Even though you feel especially alone in the pain of grief, God is with you.

Prayer: God, in the loneliness of my grief, I know that that you are here, enfolding me with the grace of your abiding Spirit. I thank you that I am not alone. Amen.

Assurance: **I relieve my loneliness when I reach out to God and to others.**

Day 2

"Let me alone, that I may find a little comfort."
Job 10:20 NRSV

Thought: Loneliness is the overarching experience of grief. When you find yourself suddenly without your loved one, loneliness is likely the pervasive condition of your heart. For a while, loneliness may be the steady, ice-cold companion of grief. Your impulse may be to both isolate and insulate yourself because you are lonely. For a while, you may want others to leave you alone so that you can grieve privately and find your own comfort. Allow yourself time alone to grieve.

Prayer: God, I am so lonely without the one lost to my life. Yet I need to be alone for a time to grieve in your comfort. Soothe the loneliness of my broken heart. Amen.

Assurance: **I will know when I am ready to reconnect.**

Day 3

"Let me alone; my days have no meaning."
Job 7:16 NIV

Thought: Your response to grief and loneliness may be utter dejection. Loneliness can drive you to a solitary place deep within. The loneliness of grief can leave your spirit tear-stained and aching. You may prefer to be alone for a while to consider your life and its meaning. Faith assures you that all of life does have meaning. Listen for God's voice within the silence of your grief.

Prayer: God, I falter in my spirit; I want to be alone. I question whether my life has meaning without my loved one. I listen for your voice within my loneliness. Amen.

Assurance: **My life does have meaning.**

Day 4

I lie awake;
I am like a lonely bird on the housetop.
Psalm 102:7 NRSV

Thought: Perhaps, like the psalmist, you lie awake, acutely aware of the absence of your loved one. You listen for familiar sounds but, instead, there is silence. You feel like a small bird on a housetop, lonely yet still with a view to the world. Your loneliness stands in sharp contrast to life going on all around you. Yet in your loneliness there is great comfort in the teaching of Christ: "Look at the birds of the air; they neither sow nor reap nor gather into barns, and yet your heavenly Father feeds them. Are you not of more value than they?" (Matthew 6:26 NRSV)

Prayer: God, because of my grief, I feel like an onlooker to life. I lie awake thinking, reliving, imagining how life should be "if only." You provide for every lonely bird viewing life from a housetop. For now, I am that lonely bird. Amen.

Assurance: **God watches over me and takes care of me.**

Day 5

We do not live to ourselves, and we do not die to ourselves.
Romans 14:7 NRSV

Thought: You do not live in a spiritual vacuum, even in grief. Though you are lonely, you neither live nor die in isolated self-sufficiency. Part of the loneliness of grief is the urgent desire to keep your loved one alive in your heart and mind. You feel the need to talk and invoke his or her name and continuing spiritual presence. You want to hear others speak with passion about the life and enduring legacy of your loved one. But who is listening, really listening? Who understands your loneliness and pain? There is someone waiting to listen to you who will understand the loneliness of your heart.

Prayer: God, I know that you understand my loneliness and pain. I live unto you, even as I express my emotional isolation to others so that you may work through their listening to help me live. Amen.

Assurance: **There is someone near who cares and wants to listen to me.**

Day 6

*The widow who is really in need and left all alone puts her hope in God and
continues night and day to
pray and to ask God for help.*
1 Timothy 5:5 NIV

Thought: Whether you have lost a spouse or another loved one, there is no doubt
that you are really in need and left all alone. Loneliness is that place of emotional
aloneness created by death and grief. While there are no quick remedies, spiritual
perseverance will lead you away from your loneliness. Hope in God, continue to
pray, and ask God for help. God answers. God will help you.

Prayer: God, I feel that I have been left all alone by the death of my loved one. I
am really in need of your presence. I hope in you; I pray for your help. Amen.

Assurance: **I will pray both night and day.**

Day 7 – Rest for Your Soul

"I will never leave you or forsake you."
Hebrews 13:5 NRSV

Thought: The effect of loneliness is the feeling of having been forsaken. The one
you grieve left you physically, yet the spirit of that person's life and love remains
with you always. Rest today from your loneliness. Extend your heart to peace
and oneness within yourself.

Prayer: God, thank you for the promise that you will never leave me or forsake
me. Your presence with me this day is rest for my soul. Amen.

Assurance: **In my loneliness I am aware of the loving presence of God.**

Week 3 – Suffering

Day 1

*For the LORD has comforted his people,
and will have compassion on his suffering ones.*
Isaiah 49:13 NRSV

Thought: Grief is suffering. The more sensitive you are, the more you suffer. If
you did not love, you would not suffer. When you grieve, you suffer the pain of

loss. Physical suffering can be a manifestation of grief as well. Grief and suffering are relieved by the comfort and compassion of God.

Prayer: God, suffering is so painful. Yet I feel your care as you comfort my spirit with the gift of your compassion. Amen.

Assurance: **God is with me in and through my suffering.**

Day 2

Are any among you suffering? They should pray.
James 5:13 NRSV

Thought: You may answer, "Yes, I am suffering!" You suffer because you have loved and lost perhaps the most important person in your life. You may withdraw and become less communicative for a while. You may question your strength and faith. You suffer as long as there is pain. With unadorned spiritual forbearance, name your suffering in the vocabulary of grief, and pray.

Prayer: God, I am suffering. I am in pain. I pray that through suffering I may find my deepest experience of your presence. Amen.

Assurance: **Suffering is relieved by prayer.**

Day 3

Therefore, let those suffering in accordance with God's will entrust themselves to a faithful Creator, while continuing to do good.
1 Peter 4:19 NRSV

Thought: In grief you may wonder whether your life is to be only about long-suffering. If you believe that it is not God's intention that you suffer forever, consider how you might help yourself through the suffering of grief. When you extend yourself in goodness to someone in need, your suffering is relieved, at least in that moment. It is true that in giving you receive and in selflessness you find.

Prayer: God, I entrust myself to you. Despite my own suffering, may I seek to do good as I wait on you, faithful Creator. Amen.

Assurance: **I will not always suffer.**

Day 4

We rejoice in our sufferings, knowing that
suffering produces endurance.
Romans 5:3 RSV

Thought: No one knows when your suffering will be over. Grief does not concede to those urging you to move on. Those who insist that you get on with your life do not appreciate that you may never "get over" your grief. When at last you have endured and found your way to the other side of pain and sorrow, you realize that it is through suffering that you better understand the things that really matter: faith, hope, and love.

Prayer: God, I am grateful that suffering teaches endurance and perseverance in life. Though it is difficult to rejoice, I trust your divine instruction. Amen.

Assurance: **Suffering is part of life. I will rejoice that I am alive.**

Day 5

But those who suffer he delivers in their suffering;
he speaks to them in their affliction.
Job 36:15 NIV

Thought: Job is the model for suffering; "the patience of Job" is a modern idiom. Job patiently suffered affliction, yet he was not entirely passive. He wanted to know the reason; he wanted to know the "why" of his suffering. In grief you may seek in vain for the "why" of death. Because of his suffering, Job learned to listen and to trust God. Listen for God speaking to you in your affliction.

Prayer: God, like Job, I want to know "why." I listen; you speak. You answer that I am not supposed to know the "why" of death. Help me to listen. Deliver me in my suffering. Amen.

Assurance: **When my rampant emotions run their course and gradually subside, my suffering will moderate.**

Day 6

And after you have suffered for a little while, the God of all grace, who has
called you to his eternal glory in Christ, will himself restore, support,
strengthen, and establish you.
1 Peter 5:10 NRSV

Thought: God calls you to draw near in order to restore, support, and strengthen you in your physical and spiritual suffering. Suffering invites you to place your hurt in larger hands, in God's hands. It may be in suffering that you determine whether your faith is a superficial ornament of life or the essential foundation on which all of life is built. Your suffering may be the source of some of the great revelations of life.

Prayer: God, what is "a little while"? Thank you for the assurance that my suffering will one day be over. Support and strengthen me this day, I pray. Amen.

Assurance: **Suffering may leave an indelible mark on my soul because it is part of the human experience.**

Day 7 – Rest for Your Soul

Rejoice in hope, be patient in suffering, persevere in prayer.
Romans 12:12 NRSV

Thought: There is relief from suffering when you persevere in prayer. In grief there are times when there are no other words than, "Lord, help me" (Matthew 15:25 NRSV). Find rest for your soul this day in the assurance that God understands your grief. God is never threatened by your feelings and emotions, especially those of grief. Be patient in suffering.

Prayer: God, this day I rejoice in hope as I lay aside suffering and pray that my soul may find its rest in you. By your grace may I be patient in suffering even as I persevere in prayer. Amen.

Assurance: **Loss and survival inspire me to greater compassion for the suffering of others.**

Week 4 – Comfort

Day 1

"Blessed are those who mourn, for they will be comforted."
Matthew 5:4 NRSV

Thought: As your grief progresses through the pain of loss and loneliness, the counterintuitive promise of the fourth beatitude or "declaration of blessedness" from the Sermon on the Mount assures you that, because you mourn, you will be blessed. In grief you may struggle to reconcile feeling blessed with mourning. After all, who feels blessed when someone dies? And what is the blessing of death for those of us who remain in this world except the end of mortal pain and suffering for the one we loved? Because mourning is the expression of your inmost sorrow, grief insists that you mourn before you are blessed with authentic comfort. Take heart. Because you mourn, you will be comforted.

Prayer: God, at this moment I am in too much pain to understand how I am blessed by my sorrow. Help me to believe the promise that I will be comforted. Amen.

Assurance: **When I am comforted, I am blessed.**

Day 2

As a mother comforts her child,
so I will comfort you.
Isaiah 66:13 NRSV

Thought: If you are a parent or if, as a child, you had someone in your life who poured out comfort to you, you have had the human experience of unconditional love. This is the love of God's comfort for you as you grieve. God's comfort goes beyond a promise. It is an absolute assurance of God's understanding presence and all-embracing comfort and care for you, especially in grief. God will comfort you.

Prayer: God, I identify with a loving parent's comfort poured out for a child in need. I am still that child in need of your comfort for my sorrowing soul. Amen.

Assurance: **I know the warmth of God's comforting love.**

Day 3

Let your steadfast love become my comfort.
Psalm 119:76 NRSV

Thought: God uses grief to teach you more of God's comfort through the constancy of steadfast love. You suffer for a while, yet you are assured of God's love as God comforts you. The unimaginable depth and breadth of God's infinite love becomes your comfort in grief.

Prayer: God, you are everlasting, even as I am becoming. Your divine love is sufficient for my comfort in grief. Amen.

Assurance: **The steadfast love of God is my comfort.**

Day 4

In the day of my trouble I seek the Lord;
in the night my hand is stretched out without wearying;
my soul refuses to be comforted.
Psalm 77:2 NRSV

Thought: In grief you learn to understand your would-be comforters, those who try to console you with empty words or gestures. You expect others to know what you are feeling, but it is not possible. For a while your soul may refuse to be comforted. You alone appreciate the depth of your personal experience of grief. The truth is that no one can comfort you to your expectations; nor can you grieve to the expectations of another. Grief is not a job with a performance standard. Comfort is yours to reject or receive.

Prayer: God, this is surely the day of my trouble. I seek you in the dark night of grief. Give me strength to seek your comfort with tireless, outstretched hands and heart. Amen.

Assurance: **As I grieve, I am comforted by the presence of God.**

Day 5

Who is like you, God? Though you have made me see troubles, many and bitter,
you will restore my life again; from the depths of the earth you will again bring
me up. You will increase my honor and comfort me once more.
Psalm 71:19-21 NIV

Thought: Comfort is not a one-time fix. In grief, your need is for repeated comfort—again and yet again. With each expression of comfort, you experience a momentary peace. Comfort relieves your pain; comfort affirms and restores your life. Comfort brings you up again from the depths of grief.

Prayer: God, as you comfort me anew each day, I am grateful that you build me up, even as you restore my life. Amen.

Assurance: **Comfort builds on comfort; comfort grows from comfort.**

Day 6

This is my comfort in my distress,
that your promise gives me life.
Psalm 119:50 NRSV

Thought: Comfort means "with strength." To be comforted is to be made strong. In the distress of grief, your comfort and strength are from the Holy Spirit, who is your great Comforter. Grief is a part of life. For a while it may become your life. In comfort you are strengthened; through comfort you have life.

Prayer: God, even as you comfort me in my distress, I claim your promise of life. Thank you for the gift of the great Comforter. Amen.

Assurance: **In comfort there is strength; in strength there is life.**

Day 7 – Rest for Your Soul

Now may our Lord Jesus Christ himself and God our Father, who loved us and through grace gave us eternal comfort and good hope, comfort your hearts and strengthen them in every good work and word.
2 Thessalonians 2:16-17 NRSV

Thought: When you are overwhelmed by grief, you may be truly un-comfort-able, that is, unable to receive comfort from others or from God. For a while, it is not possible for you to be comforted by anyone or anything. Your deepest desire is not for comfort as much as it is for the return of life as it was. How, then, do you open your heart to receive comfort? Rest. This day find rest for your soul in the love and grace of God, who comforts and strengthens your heart.

Prayer: God, as I rest from grief today, I pray that you will comfort my heart. I believe in your eternal comfort. May I live and rest this day in hope. Amen.

Assurance: **The power of comfort reaches beyond death.**

Perspective

The LORD. . . has sent me to bind up the brokenhearted,

. . . . .

to comfort all who mourn,
and provide for those who grieve . . .
to bestow on them a crown of beauty

instead of ashes,
the oil of joy
instead of mourning,
and a garment of praise
instead of a spirit of despair.
Isaiah 61:1-3 NIV

Thought: A friend wrote these words to me on an especially difficult day: "I felt your pain today. I knew I had no words to reach your emptiness...no way to break through the isolation of your grief...but I care deeply." Through the pain of grief—worry, loneliness, suffering—your source of spiritual comfort is the Holy Spirit, who binds up the brokenhearted, comforts all who mourn, and provides for those who grieve.

Prayer: God, I understand better the pain of grief. May I be open to exchanging the ashes of my sorrow for the gift of your comfort. Amen.

Assurance: **When I am ready, beauty, joy, and praise await my heart.**

Grief Is Pain

_____

_____

_____

_____

_____

_____

_____

_____

_____

_____

_____

_____

_____

_____

_____

_____

_____

_____

GRIEF IS WORK

On the inside, I was a rigid knot of tension, frustration, and hope-lessness—with grief at my very core. I tried to untangle a few threads slowly and thoughtfully, but the maze seemed too deep and too dense. I did not know how to go on or how to live again. In my chronic state of despair, I felt at the very edge of unraveling completely—throwing in, giving up. I did not know what I should "do" to make life any better or different except to persevere in the hope—a most elusive gift—that one day, someday my life would be and feel better. I felt conflicted, at war within myself. The battle raged between trust and faith and despair. The struggle goes on. Though my life feels damaged, it is not permanently disabled by death.

Preparation

"Come to me, all you that are weary and are carrying heavy burdens, and I will give you rest. Take my yoke upon you, and learn from me; for I am gentle and humble in heart, and you will find rest for your souls. For my yoke is easy, and my burden is light."
Matthew 11:28-30 NSRV

Thought: Grief is work. It is a full-time job. For a while it seems like a 24/7 occupation. It is physically exhausting to grieve. The things of this world necessitate physical chores that may layer your grief with fatigue. Duties and responsibilities once shared with another may now be yours alone. Grief demands your energy. Grief appropriates your personal reserves and depletes your emotional resources. When grief is at the forefront of your every thought and action, it is almost unimaginable to think about letting it go. You work at it; then you rest.

Prayer: God, I am weary from the heavy load of grief. Thank you for inviting me to work beside you so that I may learn from you the life lessons of grief. Amen.

Assurance: **Grief is hard work. I must remember to rest.**

Week 1 – Victimization

Day 1

But you, God, see the trouble of the afflicted;
you consider their grief and take it in hand.
The victims commit themselves to you;
you are the helper of the fatherless.
Psalm 10:14 NIV

Thought: Victimization may be a place on the journey through grief where you reside for a while. With the death of your loved one, you become a victim through no action of your own. Because death is permanent loss, all you love and hold dear may seem irreparably damaged. You feel helpless against the effect of death on your life because your emotional, physical, and spiritual reserves are compromised and drained by the demands of grief. For a while you are a victim, focused only on the pain of grief. But as your helper, God takes your grief in hand.

Prayer: God, I am afflicted; you see my trouble. I commit myself to your care. You are my helper, the helper of all who grieve. Amen.

Assurance: **God holds my grief in large, capable hands.**

Day 2

The LORD struck the child that Uriah's wife bore to David, and it became very ill. David therefore pleaded with God for the child; David fasted, and went in and lay all night on the ground.
2 Samuel 12:15-16 NRSV

Thought: The biblical narrative for the next five days describes the victimization and incipient grief of David, an acclaimed warrior, musician, and poet of many psalms. The actions of David at the illness and subsequent death of his beloved son may remind you of your struggle through grief. When you are a victim, you act and react, especially when calamity strikes your life. Perhaps, like David, you pleaded with God to spare the life of your loved one or to reverse the circumstances in some way. It is likely that the ground of David's resting place was cold, hard, and dirty—perhaps not unlike the uncomfortable sofa or hospital recliner that may have been your resting place for days or weeks. In the identity of David, God speaks to you through this story about the human experience of death and grief.

Prayer: God, grief is so real yet so abstract. Thank you for the story of David. His response to victimization enlightens my own. Amen.

Assurance: **I trust God's plan for life.**

Day 3

On the seventh day the child died. And the servants of David were afraid to tell him that the child was dead; for they said, "While the child was still alive, we spoke to him, and he did not listen to us; how then can we tell him the child is dead? He may do himself some harm."
2 Samuel 12:18 NRSV

Thought: The fear and dread expressed by the servants may remind you of a doctor, nurse, hospice worker, or family member who was reluctant to be the herald of bad news. Were others protecting you from death? Were they afraid to tell you the truth? Were they fearful for you? Perhaps you reacted with anger. Perhaps you succumbed to a sense of overwhelming defeat and powerlessness. You may feel abandoned by God or by the one who died. Likely you were unprepared to manage your victimization. The work of grief honors your season of victimization.

Prayer: God, it is hard work to be a victim. I do not understand what happened and, like David, I did not want to hear the news of death. But I know that through your grace, death does not have the last word in life. Amen.

Assurance: **My sense of abandonment is a real part of my victimization.**

Day 4

But when David saw that his servants were whispering together, he perceived that the child was dead; and David said to his servants, "Is the child dead?" They said, "He is dead."
2 Samuel 12:19 NRSV

Thought: David was not spared the harsh reality of death. No one relied on the euphemisms of death—"He passed away," "He's gone," "He's not with us anymore"—to communicate the truth to David. Likely you were affected by the words that were used to express the fact of the death of your loved one, as well. "He is dead." "She is dead." Often these words signal the onset of grief.

Prayer: God, death is so harsh. There are no comfortable words to make it less so. You promise that in death there is life. I am assured even though I grieve. Amen.

Assurance: **When there are no answers to the mystery of life and death, I look within to what I believe.**

Day 5

Then David rose from the ground, washed, anointed himself, and changed his clothes. He went into the house of the LORD, and worshiped; he then went to his own house; and when he asked, they set food before him and he ate.
2 Samuel 12:20 NRSV

Thought: David reached the turning point in victimization. After he was told that the child was dead, he took action. He got up from the ground. David then anointed himself with lotion and put on some fresh clothes. He took time to take care of himself. He took the first step to prepare for the rest of his life without his beloved child. In that moment he moved from victim to survivor.

Prayer: God, the inertia of victimization sustains my grief. Like David, may I have the spiritual strength to worship you from my wounded heart. Amen.

Assurance: **My worship acknowledges the power of God in life and death.**

Day 6

"While the child was still alive, I fasted and wept; for I said, 'Who knows? The LORD may be gracious to me, and the child may live.' But now he is dead; why should I fast? Can I bring him back again? I shall go to him, but he will not return to me."
2 Samuel 12:22-23 NRSV

Thought: Uncharacteristic behavior is part of grief. It is, in fact, an inalienable right of grief. You may feel irrational or scarcely sane. You are not yourself. It is not unusual to weep uncontrollably and reject the comfort of others. Perhaps you refuse to take care of yourself. The narrative suggests that David returned to his routine easily and quickly. More likely, the biblical timeline of events is abridged. However, as his grief subsided, it is clear that David gradually resumed a semblance of normalcy. David knew with certainty that the child would not return to him. He was equally certain that he would be with the child again. David affirmed his faith in eternal life.

Prayer: God, I am encouraged by the example of David. Like him, I trust in your compassionate care for me. Amen.

Assurance: **I will be reunited with those I love who have died.**

Day 7 – Rest for Your Soul

I will not die, but live. . . .
The LORD . . . has not given me over to death.
Psalm 118:17-18 NASB

Thought: When you consciously resolve to survive, your choice is surviving day to day or surviving for life. If you are empowered rather than debilitated by the experience of life and death, you want to survive—to be a Survivor with a capital S. Moving from Victim to Survivor is a milestone in grief. You are no longer a victim; rest this day as a grateful Survivor. Meditate on the fullness of life.

Prayer: God, I choose to be a Survivor. You have not given me over to death. Your grace assures me that I will live through grief. Amen.

Assurance: **Moving from Victim to Survivor is a personal triumph.**

Week 2 – Despair

Day 1

Yet God prolongs the life of the mighty by his power;
they rise up when they despair of life.
Job 24:22 NRSV

Thought: Grief is despair in response to the emotional upheaval of death. Despair is the dark side of grief. It is a place of emotional surrender as you journey through the valley of the shadow of death. When you despair of life, you may drift unaware into cynical acceptance or defeated resignation. Grief assails your hope; without hope you despair. By the power of God you are raised up from despair.

Prayer: God, you alone are mighty. By your power, prolong my life beyond today that I may rise up from despair. Amen.

Assurance: **The antidote to my despair is hope.**

Day 2

Insults have broken my heart,
so that I am in despair.
I looked for pity, but there was none;
and for comforters, but I found none.
Psalm 69:20 NRSV

Thought: Death is an insult that breaks the human heart. The death of your loved one has left you bereft, perhaps in complete despair. Is pity really what you desire in grief? No, you seek the Comforter to lead you away from despair and teach you again of hope.

Prayer: God, death has broken my heart. In the grace of your love I know that you pity the frailty of my despair. May I hope in your comfort. Amen.

Assurance: **I will forsake despair and learn again of hope.**

Day 3

I have not run away from being your shepherd;
you know I have not desired the day of despair.
Jeremiah 17:16 NIV

Thought: God never runs away from you, especially when you grieve. You may run from God, but God is always here for you. The mission of a shepherd is to lead and guide the way. A shepherd's job is to ensure protection and safe passage. The shepherd desires nothing less than complete safety for the flock. As you grieve, remember that God is here. God has not run away. Do not despair.

Prayer: God, you are my shepherd. I know that my despair is not your desire. Hear my heart as I seek you in prayer. Amen.

Assurance: **I am in the care of a loving Shepherd.**

Day 4

We were under great pressure, far beyond our ability to endure,
so that we despaired of life itself.
2 Corinthians 1:8 NIV

Thought: Grief creates great pressure in your life. You feel pressured by others who say, "You've got to get on with your life." Societal pressures urge you to re-join life before you have fully engaged with your loss, because the world is not waiting on you, or for you. In grief you encounter the pressure of new responsibilities. When pressure seems beyond your ability to endure, your inclination may be to despair of life itself. Pressure is unsustainable. Your despair finds its best release through the spiritual outlet of prayer.

Prayer: God, you know the pressure I experience every day in all things large and small. Pressure seems magnified by my grief. I pray for the ability to endure. Fortify my soul and spirit that I do not despair of life itself. Amen.

Assurance: **I know that, with God's strength, I have the ability within to endure through grief.**

Day 5

Listen to my cry,
for I am in desperate need.
Psalm 142:6 NIV

Thought: Desperation is the active internalization of despair. This extreme expression of despair can result in dire consequences. If you are living in emotional darkness, overwhelmed by negativity and immobilized by grief, ask for help. Find a confidential, non-judgmental counselor, therapist, or minister who will listen thoughtfully and understand your grief. Let another guide you away from despair into the light.

Prayer: God, listen to my cry, for I am in desperate need. Calm the despair of my heart. I seek your wisdom and counsel. Amen.

Assurance: **The desperation caused by my grief will not last forever.**

Day 6

Why are you in despair, O my soul?
And why have you become disturbed within me?
Hope in God, for I shall again praise Him,
For the help of His presence.
Psalm 42:5 NASB

Thought: Grief is about so many questions: "Why?" "Why me?" "Why didn't God answer my prayers for healing?" "Why did this have to happen?" "Why did he or she have to die (and not me)?" "How can I go on without my loved one?" These are the questions of despair that disturb and roil your soul. Answers are elusive—some you figure out by logic and reasoning; some become clear over time. For others, there simply are no answers. Hope in God.

Prayer: God, in your infinite grace, you answer me and save me from despair. I praise you, for you are my help and my God. Amen.

Assurance: **Because God is my hope and my help, I am stronger than I even imagine.**

Day 7 – Rest for Your Soul

May your unfailing love be with us, O LORD,
even as we put our hope in you.
Psalm 33:22 NIV

Thought: On this day of rest from grief, meditate on the unfailing love of God. God's love is with you. God's unfailing love is larger than despair. It conquers desperation and calms whatever disturbs your spirit. Rest today in the love of God, which never fails you.

Prayer: God, thank you for your eternal, unfailing love that is with me this day and every day. I pray for rest for my soul as I put my hope in you. Amen.

Assurance: **My soul finds rest when my despair turns to hope.**

Week 3 – Struggle

Day 1

You are jealous for something you can't get, so you struggle and fight. You
don't have because you don't ask.
James 4:2 CEB

Thought: In grief, what you may desire most is to have your life back. You want what is permanently gone, that which will never again be restored to your life. The struggle and fight are likely within yourself. Perhaps you struggle silently with God, reluctant to ask for God's help in your lonely uphill struggle through grief. Struggle is normal in grief and leads to growth beyond grief.

Prayer: God, I struggle and fight a daily war within myself. I know that you are not the enemy. You are my one true ally. I ask for your leadership as I concede the battle and fight only the good fight toward life in you. Amen.

Assurance: **As I struggle through grief, I grow spiritually toward life.**

Day 2

No one can comprehend what goes on under the sun. Despite all their efforts to search it out, no one can discover its meaning. Even if the wise claim they know, they cannot really comprehend it.
Ecclesiastes 8:17 NIV

Thought: You may never understand what goes on under the sun, especially on this side of heaven. You struggle with and through grief in order to survive and live again. The assumption of grief is that you are supposed to "do" something to help yourself. Effort and trying are the assumptions of doing when really all you may want to "do" is succumb to heartbreak. You struggle with the meaning of death and life. Faith is the only answer that makes sense.

Prayer: God, you are all-wise. You alone know and understand that which I will never comprehend. I question and ask. I struggle to live in you faithfully. May I do less and trust you more. Amen.

Assurance: **As I struggle to endure grief, slowly I triumph over it.**

Day 3

"I have no one to put me into the pool when the water is stirred up; and while I am making my way, someone else steps down ahead of me."
John 5:7 NRSV

Thought: At the pool of Bethesda in Jerusalem, an angel of the Lord came down from time to time to stir up the waters. The first one into the pool after each such disturbance would be cured of whatever disease he or she had. A man sitting beside the pool had been an invalid for thirty-eight years. He struggled, but he was unable to manage his infirm body into the pool by himself. His effort was not enough to get ahead of those more mobile and able-bodied. His struggle was daily and persistent, perhaps not unlike your struggle through grief. His life changed forever when Jesus asked, "Do you want to be made well?" (John 5:6 NRSV)

Prayer: God, grief seems like a persistent infirmity. I pray that your grace will break through the dailiness of my struggle. Amen.

Assurance: **Even as I struggle through grief, I know that I want to be made well.**

Day 4

"You have struggled with God and with humans
and have overcome."
Genesis 32:28 NIV

Thought: Life takes an effort, whatever the circumstance or quest. Grief demands that you make an effort in order to survive. When you struggle, you try. Trying may feel like failure or like unexpected success. In fact, trying may feel like a full-time occupation. There are no real failures when you struggle and try.

Prayer: God, I struggle with others who do not understand my grief. I struggle with you as I seek to overcome my resistance to life without the one I love. May your Holy Spirit prevail in my heart. Amen.

Assurance: **Every small victory in grief is progress.**

Day 5

We work and struggle for this:
"Our hope is set on the living God,
who is the savior of all people,
especially those who believe."
1 Timothy 4:10 CEB

Thought: You struggle, compelled every day to do the hard work of grief again and yet again. You "try on" new ways to live, perhaps alone for the first time in life. You "try out" new people. You try to adapt to the expectations of others. You try new experiences. You try to go on with life. All the work and struggle of grief are for this: hope.

Prayer: God, my hope is set on you, the living God. Though I struggle and, at times, feel dead, I believe that you save me unto life. Amen.

Assurance: **I hope and believe.**

Day 6

He gives strength to the weary
and increases the power of the weak.
Isaiah 40:29 NIV

Thought: Even under the best circumstances, it is exhausting to struggle with anything or anyone. Yet trying is an obligation of grief. But there is no guarantee that effort alone will ease the void once filled by the love and energy of your loved one. It will always matter to you that you have loved and lost; it will never not matter. You must struggle and try in order to survive.

Prayer: God, I now understand more about the cause and effect of my struggle. I am weak and weary from the effort to defend my sorrow. I am grateful for the sustaining strength and power of your love and grace. Amen.

Assurance: **Struggle moves me from the defensiveness of grief to quiet confidence and renewed self-assurance.**

Day 7 – Rest for Your Soul

"I know your works, your toil and
your patient endurance."
Revelation 2:2 NRSV

Thought: You struggle, you persevere, you endure through the pain of grief. Rest today in the certainty that your work and emotional toil are not in vain. "For this I toil and struggle with all the energy that he powerfully inspires within me" (Colossians 1:29 NRSV). Claim the energy and power of God's inspiration this day and every day.

Prayer: God, it is good to rest from the ongoing struggle of my grief. I am encouraged, for you know my works, my toil, and my patient endurance. May I live refreshed in your energy and power as I seek rest for my soul in you today. Amen.

Assurance: **I win the struggle when I acknowledge that my life is here and now.**

Week 4 – Stress

Day 1

No testing has overtaken you that is not common to everyone. God is faithful, and he will not let you be tested beyond your strength, but with the testing he will also provide the way out so that you may be able to endure it.
1 Corinthians 10:13 NRSV

Thought: Grief is the stress of sorting out life before going forward again. Stress is hardship. Stress is adversity. Stress is a force that tests both your strength and your ability to withstand it. Stress is everywhere in contemporary society. The stress of grief is multidimensional and real. The promise of grief is that you will not be tested beyond your strength.

Prayer: God, the death of my loved one severely tests my physical and spiritual stamina. You know my weakness and my limitations. Thank you that I am not tested beyond my strength. Amen.

Assurance: **God is faithful and will provide the way out of my grief.**

Day 2

So we do not lose heart. Even though our outer nature is wasting away, our inner nature is being renewed day by day. For this slight momentary affliction is preparing us for an eternal weight of glory beyond all measure.
2 Corinthians 4:16-17 NRSV

Thought: Grief causes stress on your mind, body, heart, and soul. Stress is often an involuntary response to anything that upsets your personal balance. The death of your loved one is likely among the most stressful experiences of your life. Stress disrupts your emotions with its irrationality and insistence. Yet you are assured that stress is but a slight momentary affliction to be endured while your inner nature is being renewed day by day.

Prayer: God, it is almost impossible to imagine an eternal weight of glory beyond all measure. In your strength may I look to that which cannot be seen, that which is eternal, for relief from the affliction of my grief. Amen.

Assurance: **I do not lose heart.**

Day 3

When they call to me, I will answer them;
I will be with them in trouble,
I will rescue them and honor them.
Psalm 91:15 NRSV

Thought: The stress of grief can affect your physical health. A man in the hospital as the result of a heart attack received a call from a concerned staff member at his church. She asked whether the stress of grief for his recently deceased wife might be contributing to his condition. He had not seriously thought of this as a possibility. The question caused him to consider how grief might have physical consequences as well as its known effects on the spirit. God promises to deliver you. God promises to protect you. God promises to answer you. God promises to be with you in trouble. God knows the effect of stress as you grieve.

Prayer: God, I am grateful for your promise to rescue me. Today life is especially stressful because of the death of my loved one. You honor me with your faithfulness; I trust you to satisfy my soul. Amen.

Assurance: **God answers when I call.**

Day 4

Where can I go from your spirit?
Or where can I flee from your presence?
. . . .
If I take the wings of the morning
and settle at the farthest limits of the sea,
even there your hand shall lead me,
and your right hand shall hold me fast.
Psalm 139:7, 9-10 NRSV

Thought: The psalmist expresses the urge to flee—a typical reaction to stress. Examine your thoughts for these signs of stress: Do you have trouble sleeping? Do you overeat or have no appetite? Do you worry constantly? Do you have increased heart rate or rapid breathing while at rest? Are you irritable, angry, or impatient? Are you tired? Are you unable to concentrate? It is God's hand that leads you through the stress of grief.

Prayer: God, when stress overwhelms me, I want to run away and hide from everything, even from you. I am grateful that there is nowhere beyond your reach and protection. Amen.

Assurance: **God's care for me extends to the farthest limits of the sea.**

Day 5

Now as they went on their way, he entered a certain village, where a woman named Martha welcomed him into her home. She had a sister named Mary, who sat at the Lord's feet and listened to what he was saying. But Martha was distracted by her many tasks; so she came to him and asked, "Lord, do you not care that my sister has left me to do all the work by myself? Tell her then to help me." But the Lord answered her, "Martha, Martha, you are worried and distracted by many things; there is need of only one thing. Mary has chosen the better part, which will not be taken away from her."
Luke 10:38-42 NRSV

Thought: The story of Mary and Martha is a biblical paradigm for modern-day stress. Martha welcomed Jesus into their home and busied herself with the work of hospitality. Mary sat at the Lord's feet and listened to what he said. Martha stressed because her sister left her to do all the work by herself. She was distracted by her many tasks, just as we are today. Martha was, in fact, a stress carrier. She complained in the name of sibling justice because she wanted Mary to share the load. Mary chose the better part.

Prayer: God, I stress over the duties and responsibilities of life, especially now that I am without my loved one. May I be like Mary and choose the better part—to be in your presence. Amen.

Assurance: **Today I choose the better part, which cannot be taken away from me.**

Day 6

*When I thought, "My foot is slipping,"
your steadfast love, O LORD, held me up.
When the cares of my heart are many,
your consolations cheer my soul.*
Psalm 94:18-19 NRSV

Thought: In stress you may cry, "My foot is slipping." The wisdom of the ages, anecdotal reports, numerous clinical studies, and sophisticated tests confirm that strong social and emotional support systems offer relief from stress. Social support improves health and prolongs life. The steadfast love of God holds you up in grief. God knows the cares of your heart.

Prayer: God, in the stress of grief, the cares of my heart are, indeed, many. Thank you for the consolation of your steadfast love. Amen.

Assurance: **God's consolations cheer my soul.**

Day 7 – Rest for Your Soul

My flesh and my heart may fail,
but God is the strength of my heart and my portion forever.
Psalm 73:26 NRSV

Thought: Stress is the scientific principle of physics that explains elasticity, which allows matter to resume its original size and shape after being compressed or stretched by an external force. Grief forces you to stretch, almost to the breaking point. The principle of elasticity applies to grief: compressed or stretched by the effect of death, your spirit, in time, resumes its form and shape. Today, rest from the stress of daily life. God is the strength of your heart.

Prayer: God, when life overflows with the stress of grief, it feels as if my body and my heart may fail. May I rest in the strength of your heart today and not in my own. Amen.

Assurance: **Today I rest in the certainty that God is forever.**

Perspective

"Restrain your voice from weeping
and your eyes from tears,
for your work will be rewarded."
Jeremiah 31:16 NIV

Thought: Those who formally retire from the workplace know the sense of accomplishment from a job well done. Yet retirement is often accompanied by the unsettling randomness of finding something else in life to do. Similarly, the work of grief is the despair, the struggle, and the stress of determining where to invest your energy, time, and emotional capital—the personal resources once dedicated perhaps solely to your loved one. Know that your work will be rewarded.

Prayer: God, I am less tearful; I weep less often. I am doing the work of grief. It stretches me, it stresses me, and at times it still causes me to despair. Yet I am no longer a victim; rather, through your grace, I am a survivor. Thank you for your steadfast love and care. Amen.

Assurance: **There is reward for doing the work of grief.**

Grief Is Work

_____

_____

_____

_____

_____

_____

_____

_____

_____

_____

_____

_____

_____

_____

_____

_____

GRIEF IS GROWTH

On December 28, 1999, the usually peaceful gardens of Versailles were devastated by a powerful wind storm that uprooted more than ten thousand trees. In just two hours, over two hundred years of trees were destroyed—trees planted and cultivated since the seventeenth century. The Society of the Friends of Versailles sent an urgent solicitation for contributions to replace the trees. Leighton and I were not members of this organization, but we were certainly friends of Versailles.

In honor of Leighton's seventieth birthday in 2000, I gave a new tree for the gardens. Months later an acknowledgment came that identified the location of "his" tree in the vast park. When we visited there to celebrate our fifteenth wedding anniversary, we looked for the tree, "his" tree—a small, brave sapling, one among thousands of new specimens. We did not find it— only the general area of its habitation. There is no plaque with Leighton's name inscribed on it, only the pleasure of knowing that something new and green grows in his honor, and now in his memory. Forever?

A tree grows in a garden. And life goes on.

Preparation

For surely I know the plans I have for you, says the LORD, plans for your welfare and not for harm, to give you a future with hope.
Jeremiah 29:11 NRSV

Thought: Grief is growth. Growth is a choice. Grief offers you two possibilities. You can grow, or you can remain rooted in a physical and emotional past that no longer exists. When you resist growth, you may easily succumb to the past, spending your days in sadness, frustration, and self-pity. Growth moves you to a new place that inspires reinvestment in the future. You grow spiritually through grief when you allow the forward dynamic of faith to propel you away from the past toward the light of new life.

Prayer: God, I know that you have a plan for me. Thank you for the promise of a future with hope. Amen.

Assurance: **Life unfolds when I dare to grow.**

Week 1 – Past

Day 1

Remember the days of old,
consider the years long past.
Deuteronomy 32:7 NRSV

Thought: As growth gradually redirects your grief, you become more immersed in the positive, life-sustaining memories of your relationship with your loved one than in the unalterable fact of death. For some, it may take several years to work through profound loss and grief. There is no benefit to reliving the past by scraping back through the emotional anguish and sorrow of dying and death, because the outcome will always be the same. Reliving is unproductive grief; remembering memorializes the best of the past while cherishing the present gift of today.

Prayer: God, it is important to pause and look back to remember the past so that I may give thanks again for all that was, even as I grow into the life that will yet be. Amen.

Assurance: **The past informs the rest of the life I have been given to live.**

Day 2

For a thousand years in your sight
are like yesterday when it is past,
or like a watch in the night.
Psalm 90:4 NRSV

Thought: Your earthly life together with your loved one was real. Memories will always float up, reminding you that the past is forever a very real part of your life. Nothing can void or erase what you had in whatever lifetime you shared together. But living defensively in the present—in stalwart defense of the past—negates the defenseless future. "With the Lord a day is like a thousand years, and a thousand years are like a day" (2 Peter 3:8 NIV).

Prayer: God, your sense of time is eternal. The past seems like only yesterday, even as I grow forward through your grace. Amen.

Assurance: **The past is a sacred space in my life that will always be.**

Day 3

He has made everything suitable for its time; moreover he has put a sense of past and future into their minds, yet they cannot find out what God has done from the beginning to the end.
Ecclesiastes 3:11 NRSV

Thought: It is a milestone in grief when your perspective shifts to include both the past and the future. Perspective is the compass that points the way as you grow through grief. Time reframes what happened into how you live forward. Time allows you to reflect with more than a rearview mirror. You are sustained by your memories, a precious part of the past. You will never, ever forget that which you share forever in trust with the one lost to you in death.

Prayer: God, I do not need to understand your divine plan for all of time. Rather, I am grateful for the sense of past and future with which you bless my mind and heart. Amen.

Assurance: **My perspective now includes both the past and the future.**

Day 4

For now the winter is past,
the rain is over and gone.
Song of Solomon 2:11 NRSV

Thought: Grief is a wintry experience. It is cold, dark, and isolating. For a while it seems that the winter of grief will never pass. Then one day the worst of the storm passes. The rain is over and gone. It is in the past; it is an invisible part of the past. Perhaps some damage remains—a reminder of the forces in life—as grief passes from without and within and winter is finally past.

Prayer: God, as I grow forward, I feel the winter of grief yielding to the warm promise of new life. I am grateful that the rain is over and gone. Amen.

Assurance: **What lies behind is my history, part of who I will yet become.**

Day 5

You will forget your misery;
you will remember it as waters that have passed away.
Job 11:16 NRSV

Thought: Having been through the trauma of the death of a loved one, likely you have moments of personal pain and misery that still whisper in a corner of your heart even as life grows away from the past. Your helplessness in the face of illness and death, words said or left unsaid, and the pain and sorrow of grief can be attributed to the ebb and flow of waters that are, at last, gratefully passing away.

Prayer: God, there are thoughts of past misery that linger in my soul. I pray that those memories will pass away as waters flowing away from the horizon of my grief. Amen.

Assurance: **I can choose to live without remembering the misery.**

Day 6

From ages past no one has heard,
no ear has perceived,
no eye has seen any God besides you,
who works for those who wait for him.
Isaiah 64:4 NRSV

Thought: God is at work in your life even as you wait for God in grief. When you wait, life seems to be neither in the past nor in the present. The experience of life in suspended animation is that of always waiting for "something to happen." You may chafe at "marking time," or waiting on "the next thing." Does the past dictate the present or the future? Will there yet be life not entirely defined by what once was and will never be again? God speaks in your heart; listen for the answer.

Prayer: God, no one has ever heard or sensed or seen how you work to order the universe and the world in which we live. In faith I know that you are at work in my life. I wait for you. Amen.

Assurance: **I hold on. I let go. I grieve and grow forward into the present.**

Day 7 – Rest for Your Soul

For I am convinced that neither death nor life, neither angels nor demons, neither the present nor the future, nor any powers, neither height nor depth, nor anything else in all creation, will be able to separate us from the love of God that is in Christ Jesus our Lord.
Romans 8:38-39 NIV

Thought: By its very omission, it is profound that Romans 8:38-39 does not include the past as a force capable of separating you from the love of Christ. The past has no power over life or death or your relationship with God through Christ. You arrive at an important moment in grief when what was—the past—no longer competes with what is—the present—for meaning and purpose in your life.

Prayer: God, I rest today in new understanding that the past cannot separate me from your love. I am grateful for your tenacious grace that teaches me more of you through my grief. Amen.

Assurance: **The past was then; this is now. What happened belongs to the past.**

Week 2 – Present

Day 1

I consider that the sufferings of this present time are not worth comparing with the glory about to be revealed to us.
Romans 8:18 NRSV

Thought: The suffering you are enduring in the present needs the foundation of the past as well as the view to the future in order for you to move ahead on the journey through grief. You cherish the unforgettable, you build on the past, you hold on to all that gives value and worth to life, conformed to the reality of the present. Slowly you realize that it is possible to let go of the past and be fully in the present in one seamless emotional stand.

Prayer: God, as I release my hold on the past, the vista of the present is now more visible. I trust in the glory of the future in you. Amen.

Assurance: **What God wants is more than I can imagine.**

Day 2

*At present all I know is a little fraction of the truth, but the time will come when
I shall know it as fully as God now knows me!*
1 Corinthians 13:12 JBP

Thought: What God desires when you grieve is loyalty that does not demand full understanding. God insists on your trust even when you do not know where your pain and sorrow are leading you. The complete truth about life and death, about the past and the present, is known only to God. God knows you fully; be fully present to God.

Prayer: God, the past was then; the present is now. The complete picture of my life is known only to you. May I respond to your grace with loyalty and trust. Amen.

Assurance: **There is more to life than what I see.**

Day 3

*God is our refuge and strength,
a very present help in trouble.*
Psalm 46:1 NRSV

Thought: The present is a place as well as a time. Nothing is more comforting or life-affirming than the assurance of God's presence to help you through the trouble of grief. God's presence is reflected in the past and directed to your life here and now. Live in the present.

Prayer: God, you are my refuge and strength. You go before me; you stand beside me in the trouble of grief. May I live in your presence now and always. Amen.

Assurance: **God is very present to me today and forever.**

Day 4

*So if anyone is in Christ, there is a new creation: everything old has passed
away; see, everything has become new!*
2 Corinthians 5:17 NRSV

Thought: You are made new in grief through Christ. In the present, each new day is an opportunity to grow away from the past and into new life, your life. To move ahead, it may be necessary, though painful, to let go of unproductive people and events from the past. It makes little sense to tow with you into the present anyone or anything that has no place in your new creation. Everything is becoming new.

Prayer: God, I am in Christ; I long for new creation. Everything old has passed away. I long for newness of life. Amen.

Assurance: **I prepare for new life when I lighten my load.**

Day 5

Godliness is valuable in every way, holding promise for both the present life and the life to come.
1 Timothy 4:8 NRSV

Thought: Godliness is not always at the forefront of human thought. Yet there is perhaps no greater walk of godliness than through the valley of the shadow of death. You live in godliness when you trust God's promise for your present life and the life to come. Godliness is indeed valuable in every way as you journey through grief.

Prayer: God, I pray that the godliness you desire is somewhere within my grief-stained heart. I receive the promise of your Spirit for the present and the future. Amen.

Assurance: **Godliness is valuable in every way, especially in my grief.**

Day 6

See, now is the acceptable time.
2 Corinthians 6:2 NRSV

Thought: We live in a technology-driven day and age that insists on instant gratification and quick results—now. What is now? Now is the present. Perhaps you would like for grief to be at an end now, this very minute, this very day. But grief does not follow the calendar. It is not an on-demand experience. How long your grief lasts is an intimate process of self-determination. The end of grief is a moment of personal and spiritual resolution.

Prayer: God, I would like for the pain of grief to be over now. Yet I know that you are instructing my life in the present with each new day. Thank you for your perfect timing. Amen.

Assurance: **Though now may be my acceptable time, grief resists my direction.**

Day 7 – Rest for Your Soul

Incline your ear and hear my words,
and apply your mind to my teaching

. . . .

So that your trust may be in the LORD,
I have made them known to you today—yes, to you.
Proverbs 22:17, 19 NRSV

Thought: The weather changes. The earth is still. The air grows cold as the gray-green water of the lake roils in confused waves. The gentle noise of the wind overlays the sound of water gurgling over a nearby fountain. This is a backdrop of life that invites active listening for God's voice speaking to you. At your own place of quiet listening, reflect and trust. Be assured that on this day of rest, God speaks to you, beloved child.

Prayer: God, my soul is at rest this day in the quiet of your teaching. May I listen, hear, and meditate on you, even as you call me by name today. Amen.

Assurance: **I believe that God's words are made known to me today—yes, to me.**

Week 3 – Future

Day 1

See, the former things have come to pass, and new things I now declare;
before they spring forth, I tell you of them.
Isaiah 42:9 NRSV

Thought: Slowly you consign the past to its place of honor in your life. Gradually, though perhaps reluctantly, you begin to live more in the present than in the past. At last you can envision a tentative future. Yet the view is still somewhat obscured by the persistent questions of grief: "What is my life about without my loved one?" "Will I ever be loved again?" "Will I ever love again?" "Will my children be there to love and support me as I age?" These are the challenges of the future, for the future.

Prayer: God, you intimate the future to me with the gift of each new day, even as I yet waver between the past and the present. Grace my grief, I pray, as I dare new things. Amen.

Assurance: **God comes to me from the future**.

Day 2

As for those who in the present age are rich, command them
not to be haughty, or to set their hopes on the uncertainty of riches,
but rather on God who richly provides us with everything for our enjoyment.
They are to do good, to be rich in good works, generous, and
ready to share, thus storing up for themselves the
treasure of a good foundation for the future,
so that they may take hold of the life
that really is life.
1 Timothy 6:17-19 NRSV

Thought: The apostle Paul makes an important point, especially about a good foundation for the future. Regardless of whether or not you are among those who "in the present age are rich" in material wealth, when you grieve you ask very human questions about your financial security. "Will I have enough money to live?" "Who can I trust with my money?" "Will I have a job and be able to work?" Because the things of this world may quickly pass away, your foundation for the future is in spiritual treasure.

Prayer: God, you richly provide me with everything for my use and enjoyment. In response to your grace, may I be rich in good works, generous, and ready to share as a good foundation for the future. Amen.

Assurance: **I take hold of the life that really is life.**

Day 3

Why, you do not even know what will happen tomorrow. What is your life?
James 4:14 NIV

Thought: You do not know what will happen tomorrow. Perhaps you have a plan; perhaps you do not. Again the questions of grief may block your view to the future: "What will happen if I get sick?" "If I am physically struck down by unanticipated illness or infirmity, who will be there to take care of me?" "Where will I live if I get sick?" It is important to care for yourself, especially as you grieve. Attend to your health; do all that you can to sustain your physical self-sufficiency.

Prayer: God, you alone know what will happen tomorrow. Help me to follow you in faith so that I may know what my life is. Amen.

Assurance: **I resist the urge to borrow from the future.**

Day 4

Then Naomi said to her two daughters-in-law, "Go back, each of you, to your mother's home. May the LORD show you kindness, as you have shown kindness to your dead husbands and to me. May the LORD grant that each of you will find rest in the home of another husband." Then she kissed them goodbye and they wept aloud and said to her, "We will go back with you to your people."
Ruth 1:8-10 NIV

Thought: The entire book of Ruth is a rich tapestry of grief, love, and faith in the future. The story weaves past, present, and future through the lives of three widows, two young and one old. It relates how they responded to the loss of their husbands, and how God blessed each in a different and very personal way. Their mother-in-law, Naomi, urged the two younger women, Ruth and her sister-in law Orpah, to go back to their respective mothers' homes. Both Orpah and Ruth weep in protest, "We will go back with you to your people." Either option is going back to the past.

Prayer: God, I still strain against the urge to return to the known safety and security of the past. I pray that you will continue in kindness to me as you gently lead me toward the future. Amen.

Assurance: **When I let go of the life that once was, I live in the present and claim the future.**

Day 5

But Naomi said, "Return home, my daughters. Why would you come with me? Am I going to have any more sons, who could become your husbands? Return home, my daughters; I am too old to have another husband. . . . At this they wept aloud again. Then Orpah kissed her mother-in-law goodbye, but Ruth clung to her. "Look," said Naomi, "your sister-in-law is going back to her people and her gods. Go back with her."
Ruth 1:11-12, 14-15 NIV

Thought: Twice Naomi insisted that Orpah and Ruth return home. She reasoned with them, explaining the obvious reasons why there was no future in staying with her. Orpah understood her logic. She took Naomi's advice, kissed her, and went back home. But Ruth did not want to go back to her past life. She could not be swayed by Orpah's example. Instead, she took a step into the unknown future with Naomi and with God.

Prayer: God, yours is the care of a wise and loving parent. I listen for your voice to guide my choices as I greet the future in faith. Amen.

Assurance: **I step into the unknown future with faith in what is yet to be.**

Day 6

But Ruth replied, "Don't urge me to leave you or to turn back from you. Where you go I will go, and where you stay I will stay. Your people will be my people and your God my God. Where you die I will die, and there I will be buried. May the LORD deal with me, be it ever so severely, if even death separates you and me." When Naomi realized that Ruth was determined to go with her, she stopped urging her. So the two women went on until they came to Bethlehem.
Ruth 1:16-19a NIV

Thought: Ruth had a mind of her own. She was determined to go with Naomi and pledged her allegiance even unto death. Ruth instinctively knew what she must do to move from the past into the future. She moved away from the past, geographically and physically. Together Ruth and Naomi traveled from Moab to Bethlehem, a journey of about seven to ten days on foot. With loyalty and devotion, Ruth adopted Naomi and her family as her own. Ruth had no idea how God would bless her move toward new life in a new home.

Prayer: God, where you lead me I will go. You are my God. I trust you. Amen.

Assurance: **I expect the unexpected as I move toward the future.**

Day 7 – Rest for Your Soul

"And now, O LORD, what do I wait for?
My hope is in you."
Psalm 39:7 NRSV

Thought: Perhaps you are at once excited and challenged by the prospects of the future. On this day of rest, dream and pray for what may lie ahead. Be assured that in God, the best is yet to be.

Prayer: God, this day I meditate on the strength of those who throughout all the ages past have gone before to light the way into the future, even my future. Thank you for the encouragement of real people whose lives inspire me through your Holy Word. Amen.

Assurance: **I rest my soul today in the certainty of the future.**

Week 4 – Beyond

Day 1

"I am the true vine, and my Father is the vinegrower."
John 15:1 NRSV

Thought: If you have ever seen pictures of or visited a vineyard, you know that the actual vine plant is a remarkably sturdy creation of nature. At the peak of growth before the harvest, it supports a top-heavy load of tendrils, leaves, and grapes disproportionate to the slim stalk of the vine. After the harvest, the vines lie fallow until they are carefully stripped and the miracle of new growth begins again. Christ is the true vine; God is the vine-grower. You are the tendril that grows and bears fruit when you stay connected to the true vine.

Prayer: God, you are both vine and vine grower. I pray that you will cultivate and grow me beyond grief. Amen.

Assurance: **My growth comes from the stalk of the true vine.**

Day 2

"Abide in me as I abide in you. Just as the branch cannot bear fruit by itself unless it abides in the vine, neither can you unless you abide in me."
John 15:4 NRSV

Thought: It is impossible for a plant to grow spontaneously without the support of a root system. All living things require connection to a source of nourishment to flourish and produce. There can be no fruit without the vine. You do not grieve or grow autonomously from God, the vine-grower who nourishes and tends you, as your vine imperceptibly grows through grief.

Prayer: God, I am powerless to bear fruit in the world without you, the only source of spiritual sustenance and growth. May I abide in you this day as you abide in me always. Amen.

Assurance: **If I abide in the vine, I will grow beyond grief.**

Day 3

"I am the vine, you are the branches. Those who abide in me and I in them bear much fruit, because apart from me you can do nothing."
John 15:5 NRSV

Thought: The tender yet strong branches of a vine draw life from the stalk and bear fruit only if connected to the vine. The branches of a vine are offshoots that twist and turn in gnarly self-determination as they reach and grow. As they grow, the branches of the vine are carefully trained and trimmed for maximum yield. This is done by the one charged with tending the vines each day, the one responsible for the harvest, the loving God of your life.

Prayer: God, you are the vine; I am the branch. I yield today to your training and tending as I trust your abiding presence and care in my grief. Amen.

Assurance: **Apart from God, I can do nothing; with God, I bear much fruit.**

Day 4

"If you abide in me, and my words abide in you, ask for whatever you wish, and it will be done for you."
John 15:7 NRSV

Thought: The image of the vine and its branches suggests complete interdependency. Without the vine, there can be no fruit; without the potential for fruit, the vine is of little use. Especially in grief, your desire is to grow in faith and be fruitful. When you abide in God, you grow spiritually through grief.

Prayer: God, you know that in my heart I wish that my loved one would return to me in this life. But this is not what you want me to pray. May my greater, wiser wish be the desire of your heart for mine. Amen.

Assurance: **Through prayer I am transformed and renewed.**

Day 5

"My Father is glorified by this, that you bear much fruit."
John 15:8 NRSV

Thought: What does it mean to bear fruit? It is impossible to bear fruit without growth. If that which is planted fails to thrive, it does not blossom with the beauty of its produce. As with a ripe crop, when you grow, slowly you move beyond the horizon of your own grief toward the harvest of life in all its glorious goodness. Expect a great and bounteous harvest from the cultivation of grief.

Prayer: God, grief is slow growth. I pray that you are glorified by the fruit of my life as it is cultivated and enriched by grief. Amen.

Assurance: **My effort to grow and bear fruit glorifies God.**

Day 6

"As the Father has loved me, so I have loved you; abide in my love."
John 15:9 NRSV

Thought: Jesus teaches the power of love through analogy. He is the vine, God is the vine-grower, and you are the beloved branch. As the budding tendril waiting to bear ripe, firm fruit, depend on the root as you abide and grow in God's love for you.

Prayer: God, the beauty and power of your love is the greatest gift of life, even in the face of death and grief. May I abide in you, waiting to bear fruit. Amen.

Assurance: **God loves me with an everlasting love.**

Day 7 – Rest for Your Soul

"I have said these things to you so that my joy may be in you, and that your joy may be complete."
John 15:11 NRSV

Thought: When your loved one dies, you may feel as though all joy has died. The part of you that brimmed with love and joy for the one lost, for life, and for the future seems for a while withered, if not entirely dead. Grief is the season when your branch is dormant. Your spirit is not dead, only paused for the moment until life in its fullness is restored. Even now in unexpected pinhole moments joy dances on the other side of grief like fresh buds on the vine. Joy is the ripe, lucious fruit of grief.

Prayer: God, this day of rest is about renewal and rejuvenation while waiting for the harvest of the vine. My soul is at rest in the hope of your joy. Amen.

Assurance: **In Christ there is joy, complete joy.**

Perspective

But grow in the grace and knowledge of our Lord and Savior Jesus Christ. To him be glory both now and forever! Amen.
2 Peter 3:18 NIV

Thought: The directional arrow on a prominently displayed sign indicates that a neighborhood church has moved a few blocks north. It proclaims, "We've grown. We've moved." Simple words convey the message. With the death of your loved one, something happened that causes you to grow and move not only away from the past but also into that which is new. You grow each day into life here and now—life that is shaped by the past, life that contemplates the future with hope. Like the words on the sign, your life declares, "I've grown. I've moved."

Prayer: God, all praise and glory is yours, now and forever, for grace and knowledge in Christ. Thank you for nurturing me in my spiritual growth through grief. Amen.

Assurance: **I am growing away from the past, into the present, and forward unto the future.**

Grief Is Growth

_____

_____

_____

_____

_____

_____

_____

_____

_____

_____

_____

_____

_____

_____

_____

_____

_____

GRIEF IS ADJUSTMENT

Worry raged. As I stood by impotently and watched Leighton fight for his life during those long hospital days, I feared for him and for myself. I sensed the unalterable already defining my life. Going home to an empty house was unfamiliar and uncomfortable. I was alone, completely alone without him. Our world was ending, and I was powerless to stop it. I ferociously resisted the inevitable adjustment to utter chaos and irreversible circumstance.

The aftermath of his death left me drained and exhausted. Each day I was compelled to stop at the end of my energies, whenever that occurred. I could not push myself mentally or physically beyond the limitations of my grief. Grief demanded that I do routine business in slow motion, at a kind of mental half-speed. Because important decisions required wisdom and discernment, I could not be precipitant. So many adjustment issues seemed like failure to me because I was so accustomed to success. The persistent reality of death seemed to defy adjustment.

After months of what felt like chronic, daily adjustment, I realized that I wanted to live, to have love and joy again flood my life with blessing and abandon. I tried and tried again until, at last, grief moderated and I found space for its co-existence within my life as it grew forward.

Preparation

But this one thing I do: forgetting what lies behind and straining forward to what lies ahead, I press on toward the goal for the prize of the heavenly call of God in Christ Jesus.
Philippians 3:13-14 NRSV

Thought: Grief is adjustment. If you think about it, all of life is about constant, subtle adjustment. Intuitively you conform to circumstance. God has given you the ability to assess instantaneously practically any situation; you are innately equipped to adjust. Yet adjustment assumes monumental proportions when you grieve. You have spent all or part of your life in a relationship with your loved one—a bond physically dissolved by the event of death. In order to adjust, you are forced to press on toward the goal of life, whatever may lie ahead.

Prayer: God, in grief it is difficult to forget what lies behind. I pray for your vision as I strain forward in faith for what lies ahead. Amen.

Assurance: **My struggle to adjust may be a stubborn defense of the past, a reluctance to live in the present, or a rejection of hope for the future.**

Week 1 – Acknowledge

Day 1

So acknowledge today and take to heart that the LORD is God in heaven above and on the earth beneath; there is no other.
Deuteronomy 4:39 NRSV

Thought: Part of adjustment is acknowledgment—that is, recognizing or perhaps admitting, even owning—that the death of your loved one is permanent. No amount of wishing or desiring will ever alter this irrefutable reality. As you adjust in grief, you acknowledge that you cannot undo what happened. The death of one you love is perhaps for a while a daunting challenge to your faith. Take heart. God is in heaven above and on the earth beneath.

Prayer: God, as I grow and acknowledge the permanence of my loss, I know that no other than you understands my heart. Amen.

Assurance: **Emboldened by faith, I acknowledge both what is lost and what is left.**

Day 2

Remember today that it was not your children (who have not known or seen the discipline of the LORD your God), but it is you who must acknowledge his greatness, his mighty hand and his outstretched arm.
Deuteronomy 11:2 NRSV

Thought: When you courageously rekindle your life from the ashes of sorrow, you acknowledge by action and deed that you have not been destroyed by the death of your loved one. As you begin to live fully beyond your grief, you acknowledge with profound gratitude that the grace of God is the very essence of love at work in your life.

Prayer: God, I acknowledge your greatness. I see your mighty hand at work in my life, even as you hold my hand. I feel your outstretched arm holding me in my grief. Amen.

Assurance: **Acknowledging the grace of God is a measure of my faith.**

Day 3

"Because he loves me," says the LORD, "I will rescue him;
I will protect him, for he acknowledges my name."
Psalm 91:14 NIV

Thought: In grief it is normal to immerse yourself, even to lose yourself, for a while in self-involvement. To survive, you must sort through the myriad shifts forced upon you by the death of your loved one. This is the push and pull of adjustment; this is the first step away from the valley of the shadow of death.

Prayer: God, I love you; I acknowledge your name. You rescue and protect me from the perils of grief that assail my soul. Thank you for your faithfulness to me. Amen.

Assurance: **I gratefully acknowledge the steady presence of God as I grieve toward adjustment.**

Day 4

Let us acknowledge the LORD;
let us press on to acknowledge him.
As surely as the sun rises,
he will appear;
he will come to us like the winter rains,
like the spring rains that water the earth.
Hosea 6:3 NIV

Thought: The rhythm of the seasons is part of God's order in the world. There is something comforting in the predictability, even the reliability of winter rains and then spring rains that water the earth. Part of the adjustment of grief is finding a new rhythm to life, a new order for life without the presence of your loved one. Acknowledge God's order for your life; listen for the rhythm of God's grace.

Prayer: God, the rains come with each season to water the earth and bring new life. May the season of my life yet return to spring. Amen.

Assurance: **I receive the gift of grace as I faithfully acknowledge God.**

Day 5

*"Whoever acknowledges me before others, I will also
acknowledge before my Father in heaven."*
Matthew 10:32 NIV

Thought: You grow spiritually when you reach out with newfound compassion and understanding to acknowledge and comfort another who grieves. When you embrace others who are grieving the loss of a loved one, you offer them the support of a profound, shared experience. In your outreach you acknowledge to them the power and presence of God in grief.

Prayer: God, I acknowledge with gratitude your abiding presence in grief. May I extend your hand through mine to another who is in need. Amen.

Assurance: **When I acknowledge the power of Christ before others, Christ acknowledges me before God.**

Day 6

*Then I will also acknowledge to you
that your own right hand can give you victory.*
Job 40:14 NRSV

Thought: God not only challenges Job but also acknowledges to him that he has within himself the strength to triumph over his trials and loss. In response, Job humbles himself, acknowledges the might of God, and is blessed. For a while, grief may feel like a test of your will against God's will. But God is God—so much more than a right hand aide. When you acknowledge God and, like Job, use your God-ordained inner strength and resources to persevere through grief, you will be victorious as well.

Prayer: God, your right hand upholds me. My hand is in yours. Amen.

Assurance: **My victory over grief is a partnership with God.**

Day 7 – Rest for Your Soul

In all your ways acknowledge him,
and he will make straight your paths.
Proverbs 3:6 NRSV

Thought: If you acknowledge with praise, prayer, and thanksgiving that God alone is in charge of your life, God's promise is to show you the way back into life. God straightens the path as you journey upward out of the valley of the shadow of death, away from grief. Though grief is not a straight-line experience, pause today to appreciate the straightaway. Find rest for your soul.

Prayer: God, I give you thanks today that the path through grief is becoming more expansive with each new day. May I rest today in your vision for my path. Amen.

Assurance: **God is at work to make my path straight.**

Week 2 – Adapt

Day 1

Do not be conformed to this world, but be transformed by the renewing of your
minds, so that you may discern what is the will of God—
what is good and acceptable and perfect.
Romans 12:2 NRSV

Thought: Adjustment in grief is adapting to your environment, to others, and to life within yourself. Until the death of your loved one, your life may have been entrenched in daily routine, familiar people, and comfortable relationships. You learn through the experience of grief that you are not in control of circumstances, either in life or in death. Yet one thing you can control is your willingness to adapt. Adapting is a process of slow and, at times, laborious transformation.

Prayer: God, as grief compels me to adjust, I understand that I also must adapt my thoughts to better live in your will rather than in mine. I pray for a spirit that is good and acceptable and perfect to you. Amen.

Assurance: **When I adapt, I am transformed, and my mind is renewed.**

Day 2

All this is from God, who reconciled us to himself through Christ, and has given us the ministry of reconciliation; that is, in Christ God was reconciling the world to himself.
2 Corinthians 5:18-19 NRSV

Thought: Adapting and adjusting occur simultaneously in grief, externally and internally. In grief, you are compelled to reconcile the loss of your loved one to your life going forward. Reconciliation within yourself requires both adjusting and adapting. As the inevitable advance of adjustment proceeds on your upward climb out of the valley of the shadow of death, you adapt. You are positively reconciled to your experience of grief. Your renewed confidence then quietly becomes a force for your outreach of understanding to others who grieve.

Prayer: God, thank you for your new creation. I give you thanks that everything old is becoming new. Amen.

Assurance: **When I adapt, I awaken to this fundamental truth: life is worth living.**

Day 3

"My grace is sufficient for you, for power is made perfect in weakness."
2 Corinthians 12:9 NRSV

Thought: When you grieve, you may ask, "Where do I fit in life?" The dangling, pain-filled end of the question implies, "... without my loved one." Socially you may feel that you are perceived as "less than" because of the absence of the one lost to you in death. Through attrition you may be demoted involuntarily to the status of "second-class citizen"—someone who is not accorded a fair share of respect, recognition, or consideration. Being marginalized may create a sense of vulnerability and weakness. God's Word assures you that there is a perfect power greater than your weakness.

Prayer: God, there is no greater gift than your grace—your unearned, unmerited, and undeserved love. In the vulnerability of my grief, I pray for your power to be made perfect in my weakness. Amen.

Assurance: **When I reject inferior labels, I affirm my place in the world.**

Day 4

Therefore I am content with weaknesses, insults, hardships, persecutions, and calamities for the sake of Christ; for whenever I am weak, then I am strong.
2 Corinthians 12:10 NRSV

Thought: As you adapt and adjust, you acknowledge that, as a human being, you want to be treated with respect. When you are suddenly single or a become a parent without your beloved child, you may experience moments when you are not accorded the same respect as when you were part of the Parent Teacher Association, the dinner group, or even your Sunday school class. You may feel discounted because of your loss or emotionally defenseless when you are invited to join friends or get together with other parents you enjoyed before the death of your loved one. In these situations, you are easily wounded by the awkward insensitivity of others to your grief. It is hard work to adapt forward, away from life as it once was. This, too, is a normal part of the experience of grief.

Prayer: God, adapting is a difficult challenge because I am weak. Through your strength I will endure and adjust until grief is no more. Amen.

Assurance: **In Christ, when I am weak, then I am strong.**

Day 5

So I tell you this . . . that you must no longer live as the Gentiles do, in the futility of their thinking. They are darkened in their understanding and separated from the life of God because of the ignorance that is in them due to the hardening of their hearts.
Ephesians 4:17-18 NIV

Thought: If you sense that your heart is intractable, perhaps it is momentarily hardened by the pain of death. In that case, your grief may be described as ignorance, futility of thinking, darkness of understanding, or separation from God. You resist adjusting or adapting because your heart is hardened by the finality of death and the pain of grief. You may desire only that things stay the same. Willful resistance is futility of thinking. But even a hardened heart cannot be separated from the life of God.

Prayer: God, in moments when my heart feels hard and cold, I feel separated from you. Direct my ignorance and futility of thinking toward understanding of your love. Amen.

Assurance: **Below the grief-hardened surface of my heart is a bubbling fountain waiting to spring forth into life.**

Day 6

You were taught...to put off your old self...to be made new in the attitude of your minds; and to put on the new self, created to be like God in true righteousness and holiness.
Ephesians 4:22-24 NIV

Thought: Adapting is putting off your old self to be made new. Your old self may be a weary, emotionally tattered half-person as familiar to you as a comfortable old bathrobe. To be made new is to find a new self. You may choose to put on your new self and wear it gladly or to shrug into it with reluctance. You may try it on for size and make some adjustments before you are satisfied with the fit. The effect of grief is that it enlarges you to accommodate a new self—a different and better self. You are created to be like God.

Prayer: God, my old self is tired. Thank you for the promise that I may yet become a new self. Recreate me in your true righteousness and holiness. Amen.

Assurance: **When I put off my old self in order to be made new, I am adapting to all things becoming new.**

Day 7 – Rest for Your Soul

*Love and faithfulness meet together;
righteousness and peace kiss each other.
Faithfulness springs forth from the earth,
and righteousness looks down from heaven.*
Psalm 85:10-11 NIV

Thought: As you adjust and adapt, you slowly realize that you are a different person. Never again will you be the person you once were. The synergy of adjusting and adapting is a kind of inner balance between that which was and that which now is. Accept the new self you find within the balance of loss and acceptance, equalized by a more mature faith. Find rest for your soul today in the spiritual reconciliation of past to present with hope for the future.

Prayer: God, the beauty and symmetry of love and faithfulness, righteousness and peace reassure me that death does not have the final word in life. I rest today in you. Amen.

Assurance: **My heart urges me to live forward.**

Week 3 – Individuate

Day 1

For as in one body we have many members, and not all the members have the same function, so we, who are many, are one body in Christ, and individually we are members one of another.
Romans 12:4-5 NRSV

Thought: What does it mean to individuate? In the context of grief it means to reclaim the part of yourself given wholly and without reservation to the one loved and lost in death. Reclamation in no way diminishes your abiding love for the deceased. Rather, it affirmatively claims that love, which is multiplied and blessed by the relationship you shared, in order to reinvest in others.

Prayer: God, somewhere along life's way I seem to have lost my own identity. Teach me again who I am and what my function is as a member of your body. Amen.

Assurance: **I am still who I am.**

Day 2

Now you are the body of Christ and individually members of it.
1 Corinthians 12:27 NRSV

Thought: Developing the self-confidence to value yourself as a worthwhile, stand-alone individual is a formidable hurdle of grief. This is the process of finding yourself again apart from the context of your loved one. As you transition through grief, slowly and gradually you re-individuate. Or perhaps you truly individuate for the first time in life as you uncover your identity without reference to your loved one. When you individuate, you find yourself within the whole of life and explore possibilities beyond your own imagination.

Prayer: God, you made me like no other human being. Thank you for membership in your body. Amen.

Assurance: **I appreciate the personal, God-given qualities that are uniquely my own.**

Day 3

I have been young, and now am old,
yet I have not seen the righteous forsaken
or their children begging bread.
They are ever giving liberally and lending,
and their children become a blessing.
Psalm 37:25-26 NRSV

Thought: If you have lost your life partner, anxious moments may occur as you individuate and adjust to meet the needs of your children—or fit into the lives of adult children—who are now without a father or mother. Regardless of the ages of your children, your role as parent without the equal and opposite presence of your husband or wife is different—imperceptibly redefined. This is a kind of forced individuation. Young children and even teens may demand more of your time and energy. Grown children may perceive you as more dependent and in need of a substitute husband or wife, a role you neither desire nor want them to fulfill. You may feel ignored or hurt if they presume on your strength when, in fact, you need their support. In turn, they may feel inadequate to satisfy your emotional and physical needs. Whatever your loss, rebalancing relationships within a permanently altered family structure is an emotional complication of grief, especially as imperceptibly you continue to individuate.

Prayer: God, the structure of our family is confused by the death of the one loved and lost. I pray for your righteousness as I individuate and grow within our family. Amen.

Assurance: **Relationships are complicated; each individual family has its own dynamic.**

Day 4

"My presence will go with you, and I will give you rest."
Exodus 33:14 NRSV

Thought: Individuating is, in part, about recognizing yourself in the first person: you, yours. Did your life have value only in reference to the life of your loved one? Did making the life of another your priority—selflessly putting the comfort and needs of another before your own—qualify the value of your own life? Do you think less of your own life because it means little to you without him or her? Is life worth anything? Is it worth something? Is it worth nothing? What is the value of your life? These are the questions of individuation, the conflict of head and heart in claiming fullness of life for yourself.

Prayer: God, thank you that the promise of your presence is personal and individual. Help me to know myself again at this time of grief. Amen.

Assurance: **God best understands my individual place in the social structure of life.**

Day 5

"From everyone who has been given much, much will be demanded; and from the one who has been entrusted with much, much more will be asked."
Luke 12:48 NIV

Thought: Stewardship—being a wise manager of your individual gifts and resources—is a biblical mandate. Indeed, managing the things of this world is a worthy endeavor; but in grief you have been entrusted with gifts that transcend the material. Because you have loved and lost, you have been given the inestimable gifts of grief. Though it may not seem so, you have acquired the wisdom of understanding on your journey through the valley of the shadow of death.

Prayer: God, I know that you have entrusted to me a great sorrow and the unexpected gifts of grief. May I discern your will for the stewardship of my individual gifts. Amen.

Assurance: **No amount of money or property can compare to the gifts of my spirit.**

Day 6

For by the grace given to me I say to everyone among you not to think of yourself more highly than you ought to think, but to think with sober judgment, each according to the measure of faith that God has assigned.
Romans 12:3 NRSV

Thought: Gradually your place as a vital member of society and a contributor to humanity comes into view as you use your talents and interests to give to others. As you serve others, your gifts and graces reflect your faith. When you use your personal expertise to bless others, you go beyond yourself in grief.

Prayer: God, thank you for my individuality. May my judgment be thoughtful as I assess my place in the world and the gifts that I may offer in service to you. Amen.

Assurance: **I will not think too highly of myself, nor will I think too little of myself.**

Day 7 – Rest for Your Soul

Finally, brothers and sisters, rejoice! Strive for full restoration, encourage one another, be of one mind, live in peace. And the God of love and peace will be with you.
2 Corinthians 13:11 NIV

Thought: The journey through grief is about full restoration. Along the way, encourage others using your gifts of grief. Find your true self. Live in reconciliation with others. Today, rest from grief and find rest for your soul. Live in peace.

Prayer: God, I long this day for full restoration and peace. May my soul be at rest today in you. Amen.

Assurance: **On this day of rest I rejoice in the love and peace of God.**

Week 4 – Change

Day 1

Blessed is the man who perseveres under trial, because when he has stood the test, he will receive the crown of life that God has promised to those who love him.
. . . .
Every good and perfect gift is from above, coming down from the Father of the heavenly lights, who does not change like shifting shadows.
James 1:12, 17 NIV

Thought: Grief is adjusting to change. Death is what happened to change your life forever. When your loved one died, everything changed. In grief, you may resist every change thrust upon you. As much as you might want to contain or limit grief, the fact is that no amount of personal resolve or discipline can change the very nature of pain and heartache. You are tried and tested. Be assured that despite all the changes, God does not change.

Prayer: God, in shifting shadow moments it is still difficult to stand in your heavenly light. I pray for strength to withstand the test of grief so that I may wear again the crown of life. Amen.

Assurance: **The shadow of grief shifts toward light and life as I adjust to change.**

Day 2

Blessed be the name of God from age to age,
for wisdom and power are his.
Daniel 2:20 NRSV

Thought: The experience of death teaches you that the ordinary is precious. Through the heartache and sorrow of grief, you realize that your days together were a treasure. Like most, you want life to be as it once was. You want your life back. The hard reality of grief is that everything has changed.

Prayer: God, you are from age to age the same. I do not understand death, but I am grateful that you never change and that wisdom and power are yours. Amen.

Assurance: **Change is the way of hope and, at last, joy.**

Day 3

He changes times and seasons,
deposes kings and sets up kings;
Daniel 2:21a NRSV

Thought: Grief modulates, as do times and seasons. Gradually its power to direct your every mood and moment subsides. As you change, you begin to reframe your grief to include the steady presence of your loved one, safely ensconced forever in your heart. Despite the inevitability of change, you are sustained by your memories, now the most precious and sacred part of life together with your loved one. You will never, ever forget.

Prayer: God, time is and then passes; the seasons flow with the rhythm of nature. You, O God, are changeless and eternal. Amen.

Assurance: **Change is the constant of time.**

Day 4

He gives wisdom to the wise
and knowledge to those who have understanding.
Daniel 2:21b NRSV

Thought: Inherent in grief is its power to change you. Grief can impact you negatively or positively. Grief can leave you embittered and weaker than you were before the death of your loved one. Or it can change you into someone strong and fortified by the experience of profound loss. Grief can leave you disillusioned, or grief can change you into a person of renewed and inspired faith.

Prayer: God, only you are truly wise. I desire your wisdom and knowledge so that I may better understand your plan of change for me in grief. Amen.

Assurance: **I choose for grief to change me into someone wise rather than willful.**

Day 5

He reveals deep and hidden things;
Daniel 2:22a NRSV

Thought: The mystery of grief is change. As you grieve, deep and hidden things are revealed, perhaps even despite your desire to know. Change suggests self-examination. Change invites introspection. Change encourages the positive resolution of your guilt and regrets. "Call to me and I will answer you, and will tell you great and hidden things that you have not known" (Jeremiah 33:3 NRSV).

Prayer: God, in the silence of my heart I listen. Reveal to me the deep and hidden things that you would have me know so that I may be changed for good because of my grief. Amen.

Assurance: **Change thrives on prayer and meditation.**

Day 6

He knows what is in the darkness, and light dwells with him.
Daniel 2:22b NRSV

Thought: Rather than end the relationship with your loved one, death creates a new relationship. This eternal bond is not one of physical presence but of memory, spirit, and love. The daily challenge of grief is seeking the light of your loved one's spirit rather than abiding in the darkness of death. God is light, and in God there is no darkness at all.

Prayer: God, you alone know what is in the darkness of my heart. I know that light dwells with you and in you. May your light illuminate the darkness of my grief. Amen.

Assurance: **The light of faith is my strength, my hope, and my peace.**

Day 7 – Rest for Your Soul

For I the LORD do not change.
Malachi 3:6 NRSV

Thought: As you rest from grief today, reflect on the ways that your grief is changing and the ways in which grief is changing you. Do you see yourself as more capable, more independent, more thoughtful, and more deliberate? Be at peace today in the knowledge that change is at work in your life to enrich and bless your experience of grief.

Prayer: God, you declare with might and power that you do not change. I rest today in your eternal promise of hope. Amen.

Assurance: **My life will change for the better.**

Perspective

"In him we live and move and have our being."
Acts 17:28 NRSV

Thought: Adjustment is slow, steady progress through the journey of grief. Adjustment is, in fact, an overlay of grief. When you adjust, first you acknowledge your loss, whether consciously or subconsciously. As you adapt, you sense that your identity and your worldview have changed. After the death of your loved one, you reclaim that part of yourself invested with wholehearted love in relationship to find your individual self again. Change is the ebb and flow of life in grief and beyond. Grief is change.

Prayer: God, I live and move and am through your grace alone. Amen.

Assurance: **Adjustment is engaging in life that is good and rich and joyful.**

Grief Is Adjustment

GRIEF IS ACCEPTANCE

After Leighton's death, I was obsessed for a while with the need to understand why he died. "I want to know!" "I need to know!" were the constant themes of my chaotic thoughts. I could not really accept his death until I understood at least the medical reasons that explained the physical "why." The physiological answer to the question was simple. He got sick. Genetics and biology. Did he get sick and die because his body was old? Or was there a more compelling reason that required my in-depth understanding in order to release the questions and move forward?

I researched. In one study I read that most families have some area of physical constitution that is genetically weaker. It stated that over several generations, some family members may exhibit the same or similar symptoms in a specific part of the body and pass on this predisposition for a condition or inherited illness. This was the case in Leighton's family. His mother died of pancreatic cancer. He inherited the gene. At last I understood that this is likely why he got sick. In reflecting on the tragedy and trauma of his illness and seemingly senseless death, this is the only explanation that I could even begin to accept, if not completely comprehend.

Many well-intentioned though empty euphemisms attempt to answer the great mystery of the "why" of death. I desperately wanted to know the truth about God's will when death occurs. Is the death of one we love really God's will? How could tragic accidents, traumatic illness, or death from war and violence be the will of a loving, caring

God? Is death preordained by God to occur in a particular way at a specific time? Could I really believe the over-simplified rationalization that death occurs at one's "appointed time"? These were among the powerful spiritual questions of grief that taunted my mind and heart.

When I prayed, I paused over the words "Thy will be done" in the Lord's Prayer. For many months after Leighton's death I choked and struggled for meaning while others pushed forward apace with the recitation of the familiar, comfortable words. I know that as mortal humans we all will die to our body one day, even as I believe with certainty that the immortal soul lives on in eternity. I could accept Leighton's understanding of "Thy will be done": seeking, finding, and doing the will of God—not living in passive helplessness at the mercy of an inflictive, punitive God. Leighton believed that "Thy will be done" ought to be understood in the sense of perfect trust in the perfect wisdom and perfect love of God. In a sermon he said, "The will of God ought to be seen as that which is positive and affirmative and active in our lives. When we pray 'Thy will be done,' we are not praying for weary resignation or forced acceptance. We are not praying to be taken out of a situation, but to be able to take it and conquer it, to defeat it and overcome it."

Acceptance lies in the realization that I never will be able to fully comprehend some things. God alone understands life and death. The perspective that time and the wisdom of hindsight revealed to me is that Leighton's days here on earth were accomplished—that is, God's mission for Leighton's life in the work of his ministry was fulfilled. I accept this understanding in spiritual peace.

"I know that whatever God does endures for ever; nothing can be added to it, nor anything taken from it; God has done this, so that all should stand in awe before him. That which is, already has been; that which is to be, already is; and God seeks out what has gone by" (Ecclesiastes 3:14-15 NRSV).

Preparation

We know that in everything God works for good with those who love him, who are called according to his purpose.
Romans 8:28 RSV

Thought: Grief is acceptance. You may believe with certainty that God works in everything for good with those who love God and are called according to God's purpose. Yet you may question how the death of your loved one can possibly be for good in your life. The case for acceptance lies within the prepositions: "*in* everything God works *for* good *with* those who love him."

Prayer: God, I love you and want to live according to your purpose. I know that you are with me in everything and pray that you will continue to work to shape my life in your meaning and purpose. Amen.

Assurance: **God works *for* good; God uses my experience of death and grief to promote deeper, more profound faith.**

Week 1 – Mental

Day 1

O LORD, you have searched me and known me.
Psalm 139:1 NRSV

Thought: Acceptance is, in part, a slow metamorphosis of the mind. The mental processing of grief occurs simultaneously, though perhaps not precisely in tandem, with the physical, emotional, and spiritual acceptance of death. Acceptance is retraining your mind to accommodate both the absence and abiding presence of your loved one.

Prayer: God, you search me anew each day. You know me like no other. Enrich my mind with the peace of your presence. Amen.

Assurance: **I reach a turning point when grief releases its insistent hold on my mind.**

Day 2

You know when I sit down and when I rise up;
you discern my thoughts from far away.
Psalm 139:2 NRSV

Thought: Your thoughts determine who you are and how you live. Grief encourages a kind of conscious hyper-vigilance of the mind. When you deconstruct your subconscious walls of self-protection and live again in open, free exchange with others and the world, you arrive at acceptance.

Prayer: God, it inspires my mind and my faith to think that you know when I sit down and when I rise up. May my thoughts be pleasing in your sight from far away and within my soul. Amen.

Assurance: **Today I direct my thoughts toward the power of God's presence at work in my life.**

Day 3

You search out my path and my lying down,
and are acquainted with all my ways.
Psalm 139:3 NRSV

Thought: As you near acceptance, it is well to search the closed-off corners of your mind for the lingering remnants of grief. With the death of your loved one, it is understandable that for a while negative thoughts easily overwhelm the positive. Yet life lived in chronic negativity is life lived in darkness. Acceptance cannot penetrate darkness; it thrives on light.

Prayer: God, you are acquainted with all my ways. You know the thoughts of my mind. Lift me out of darkness into the light of your life and love. Amen.

Assurance: **God's ways guide my path.**

Day 4

Even before a word is on my tongue,
O Lord, you know it completely.
Psalm 139:4 NRSV

Thought: Words reflect the state of your soul—even those words uttered randomly from an absent or unfiltered mind. They speak of that which dwells deep within. When the thoughts of your mind find expression in words, you hear what grows inside after the death of your loved one. Acceptance speaks peace. Acceptance speaks love. Acceptance speaks gratitude for the gifts of grief.

Prayer: God, it is humbling and powerful to grasp that you know my every word, even before it is spoken. May I listen to my thoughts before I speak so that my words are at one with you. Amen.

Assurance: **The words I think and speak are a window into my soul.**

Day 5

You hem me in, behind and before,
and lay your hand upon me.
Psalm 139:5 NRSV

Thought: Your mind engages in a constant, ongoing dialogue with itself. You ask and answer; you consider and then reject. In grief it is exhausting to listen to a perpetual conversation of the mind, especially without your loved one present to respond and encourage. With acceptance you begin to speak less and listen more. "Whatever is true, whatever is honorable, whatever is just, whatever is pure, whatever is lovely, whatever is gracious, if there is any excellence, if there is anything worthy of praise, think about these things" (Philippians 4:8 RSV).

Prayer: God, in grief I am distracted by the clamor of my mind. In acceptance I feel your hand upon my heart. Amen.

Assurance: **I listen to God in the silence of acceptance.**

Day 6

Such knowledge is too wonderful for me;
it is so high that I cannot attain it.
Psalm 139:6 NRSV

Thought: On the way to acceptance, you pause perhaps for a moment to take a final backward glance. You remember how the dark sadness and sorrow of compelling grief once held you captive. On the upward side of grief, you at last see clearly where you have been and what you have been through. You are able to accept the death of your loved one because you have traveled the lonely, deserted road of the heart that is grief.

Prayer: God, you have taught me new, unimagined things about life and living through the experience of death and grief. Such knowledge is too wonderful for me. I am grateful for your loving kindness. Amen.

Assurance: **My life ahead waits only on acceptance.**

Day 7 – Rest for Your Soul

Search me, O God, and know my heart;
test me and know my thoughts.
Psalm 139:23 NRSV

Thought: Grief is about searching and testing, even to the point of mental exhaustion. The mind is wondrously made to span beyond anything humanly imaginable. It has an endless reserve of untapped spiritual energy. On this day of rest for your soul, find "neutral" for your thoughts. Rest your mind. Drift. Float. Dream. Pray. Refresh.

Prayer: God, you search me and know my heart. You test me and know my thoughts. My heart and mind seek only you on this day of rest. Amen.

Assurance: **I am at acceptance when I realize one day that I am no longer actively grieving.**

Week 2 – Physical

Day 1

I love the L*ORD*, *because he has heard my voice and my supplications.*
Psalm 116:1 NRSV

Thought: You move resolutely toward acceptance when you incorporate into your life with intention and resolve the changes that have occurred over the course of your grief. You accept that your loved one is physically gone and acknowledge this as permanent. You understand what happened and know that the outcome cannot be changed. Though you may not like it, reluctantly you accept it. You time-date a moment of acceptance, or acceptance simply occurs. As you have faithfully done in grief, you work at acceptance.

Prayer: God, especially since the death of my loved one, I have used the voice of body and heart to cry out to you for help. I am grateful for every evidence of your listening love. Amen.

Assurance: **I will consciously consider today what it means to accept.**

Day 2
Because he inclined his ear to me,
therefore I will call on him as long as I live.
Psalm 116:2 NRSV

Thought: In grief you listen intently to yourself and to God with the ear of your mind and inmost soul. Acceptance depends on how intently you listen to what grief has to say to you. Grace, courage, and wisdom are the hallmarks of acceptance. These are among the divine endowments of grief that grow your faith and accompany you into the life that yet lies ahead.

Prayer: God, you have inclined your ear to me and heard the prayers of my grief. May I call on you for as long as I live. Amen.

Assurance: **I accept the promise that there is life beyond grief because I know that there is life beyond death.**

Day 3

Gracious is the LORD, and righteous;
our God is merciful.
The LORD protects the simple;
when I was brought low, he saved me.
Psalm 116:5-6 NRSV

Thought: Everything new is an outward reflection of growing acceptance. If you buy sheets, tear out a wall, decide on a new car, or take a trip, you affirm acceptance of life as it is becoming. If you move from a family home, your physical place of daily life changes in acceptance of new life rather than loss. If you have made the decision to make a major change in life, such as returning to school, finding a new job, or remarrying, you are living in and with your acceptance.

Prayer: God, I better understand your grace and mercy in my walk through grief. Humbled and brought low by death, I give thanks that you have saved my life in your protection and love. Amen.

Assurance: **In acceptance I transcend physical loss and embrace the love that will always be in my heart.**

Day 4

For you have delivered my soul from death,
my eyes from tears,
my feet from stumbling.
Psalm 116:8 NRSV

Thought: Though perhaps it seemed so at the time, you did not die physically when your loved one died. Your purpose and destiny did not die with the one who is gone. In acceptance you reanimate to life. Acceptance redefines your self-perception as you go into the world alone. You live boldly in affirmation of life as it is, full of possibility and promise.

Prayer: God, you have delivered my soul from death. On the long journey through grief you have kept my feet from stumbling. I am grateful for life. Amen.

Assurance: **My tears celebrate love.**

Day 5

I walk before the LORD
in the land of the living.
Psalm 116:9 NRSV

Thought: There is no fast forward through grief. You may attempt great bounding strides, but grief will not be hurried. It cannot be circumvented. There is no easy detour around it. The slow, steady pace of a rhythmic walk ultimately sets the pace for the journey. Gratefully, the valley of the shadow of death leads through the land of the living.

Prayer: God, in grief I walk with my hand in yours. Thank you for your presence to me in the land of the living and for eternity. Amen.

Assurance: **My journey toward acceptance is in the land of the living.**

Day 6

I kept my faith, even when I said, "I am greatly afflicted."
Psalm 116:10 NRSV

Thought: The magnitude and intensity of your physical loss may be a life-altering encounter with your faith. Whether the death of your loved one was sudden or occurred over days or even years, when you look into affliction there is a moment of truth that has the power to either destroy or enlarge your faith. In faith you have the ultimate victory over death.

Prayer: God, you have heard my cry of affliction. Though I have faltered in my spirit, I have kept my faith. Thank you for growing me through grief. Amen.

Assurance: **I take heart in God's grace as I grow in faith.**

Day 7 – Rest for Your Soul

Precious in the sight of the LORD is the death of his faithful ones.
Psalm 116:15 NRSV

Thought: On this day of rest for your soul from grief, take comfort in the beautiful words of the psalmist. Death is more than the order of life in the sight of God. God loves and cares for all God's faithful ones in this life and in life eternal. God cares for you.

Prayer: God, I rest my soul in you today in the victory of acceptance. Thank you for the assurance that my loved one is with you, precious in your sight. Amen.

Assurance: **In acceptance I am restored and made whole again.**

Week 3 – Emotional

Day 1

"Very truly I tell you, you will weep and mourn while the world rejoices. You will grieve, but your grief will turn to joy."
John 16:20 NIV

Thought: How long does grief last? The answer to this emotional question of grief is an ongoing discovery as you confront and resolve your personal issues. By now you likely understand that grief comes and goes; it ebbs and flows. Imperceptibly you learn to live alongside it, but grief usually lasts longer than most who grieve expect. Grief will not be rushed.

Prayer: God, my head says that acceptance is the end of grief. Yet my heart needs more time and space to grieve the death of my loved one, even while the world rejoices. You know my heart. Amen.

Assurance: **I must grieve as long as I need to grieve.**

Day 2

Then he said to me, "It is done! I am the Alpha and the Omega, the beginning and the end. To the thirsty I will give water as a gift from the spring of the water of life."
Revelation 21:6 NRSV

Thought: The infrastructure of life consists of both beginning and end. Perhaps like most, you would like to control the "when" of both the beginning and end of most things in life. No more than you can control the exact moment that a child is born can you control death or the end of your grief. Each person starts at a different point in grief; likewise, the end of grief comes in a different way for each. Grief may have begun as a small wave that swelled through stages of illness, crashing onto the shores of your well-ordered life as the end of life neared. Grief may end as the tide of sorrow retreats to honor, acceptance, and hope.

Prayer: God, you are the only certain beginning and end. As my grief becomes acceptance, I thirst for the water of life. Amen.

Assurance: **When and how grief begins may affect how long my grief lasts.**

Day 3

*Wait for the LORD; be strong, and let your heart
take courage; wait for the Lord!*
Psalm 27:14 NRSV

Thought: Because grief defies an exact moment, your instinct may be to ignore it rather than enter into it. Some who have experienced the death of a loved one choose simply to hang on mindlessly until grief is over. In fact, you do not enter into grief. Grief enters into you. You move from "Why did this happen?" to "How will I go on?" You experience disbelief and shock and then the reality of life without your loved one as you move into acceptance and on toward the end of grief.

Prayer: God, I wait on you with new strength and courage. My heart waits for the end of grief even as I know you continue to teach me its wisdom. Amen.

Assurance: **Grief does not come with instructions on how long it lasts or how long I should grieve.**

Day 4

*Where, O death, is your victory?
Where, O death, is your sting?*
1 Corinthians 15:55 NRSV

Thought: You may ask, "Is there a 'shelf life' for grief?" For anyone who has experienced death in the first person, the answer is assuredly no. Figuratively, you may box up and shelve your unresolved issues for a while. But some time later, from the improved perspective of time, likely you will decide to take down the box and revisit its contents. You may look through what's there and touch it again. Perhaps you will hold it close and reexamine it. You may decide to let it go or hold onto it and put it back on the shelf. Or you may decide to file it, put it in another box of odds and ends, shred it, scrap it, or put it on a figurative bonfire and burn it. This is the only real "shelf life" that pertains to grief. Unlike well-marked packages at a supermarket, grief has no expiration date.

Prayer: God, death will not have the final word in my heart. I know the sting of grief, yet death does not claim victory in my soul. Thank you for your victory in death and in life. Amen.

Assurance: **A solemn and personal lesson of death is that I must grieve in order to live.**

Day 5

When this perishable body puts on imperishability,
and this mortal body puts on immortality, then the saying
that is written will be fulfilled: "Death has been
swallowed up in victory."
1 Corinthians 15:54 NRSV

Thought: For some, it may take several years to work through profound loss and grief. This is the "no end in sight" emotional turmoil that requires the insight of a professional. For others, there may be a defining moment such as remarriage or the birth of a child that clearly signifies the end of grief. Because your emotions do not conform to life's infrastructure, you alone will know when grief no longer demands the investment of your heart. Grief does not last a lifetime.

Prayer: God, through the promise of eternal life you assure me that death has been swallowed up in victory. Thank you for an imperishable and immortal soul. Amen.

Assurance: **I will know when my grief is at an end.**

Day 6

Weeping may linger for the night,
but joy comes with the morning.
Psalm 30:5 NRSV

Thought: For a while, grief may seem like an eternal night. As slowly grief releases its insistent hold on your life, the receding darkness of night yields to dawn. Dark clouds slowly drift and whisper away as they pass. Hope creeps imperceptibly onto the horizon as you greet the new day of the rest of your life with expectation, your soul again enlivened by the warmth of joy.

Prayer: God, you have made the night and the day so that I may live in darkness as well as in light. You know my tears in the night of my grief. And now my heart awaits the joy of morning. Amen.

Assurance: **With acceptance I resolve to give up fear, take on trust, and spend my life in gratitude rather than grief.**

Day 7 – Rest for Your Soul

I bless the LORD who gives me counsel;
in the night also my heart instructs me.
I keep the LORD always before me;
because he is at my right hand, I shall not be moved.
Therefore my heart is glad, and my soul rejoices;
my body also rests secure.
Psalm 16:7-9 NRSV

Thought: There is an interdependence of mind, body, heart, and soul that seems especially acute in grief. Acceptance is the rebalancing and fine-tuning of the God-ordained aspects of your spirit that make you unique and individual. On this day of rest for your soul, listen for the wise counsel of God.

Prayer: God, you are always before me. You hold my hand; sometimes I stop holding yours. Thank you for the security of your steadfast love. Amen.

Assurance: **My heart will one day be glad; my soul will again rejoice.**

Week 4 – Spiritual

Day 1

Even though I walk through the valley of the shadow of death, I fear no evil; for thou art with me; thy rod and thy staff, they comfort me.
Psalm 23:4 RSV

Thought: In this familiar, beloved scripture, the image is that of the shepherd guiding his sheep through many terrains and perils to reach hillside grazing and safety. The psalmist writes, "Even though I walk through the valley of the shadow of death." He uses the first person, "I." As a survivor, you have been through the valley of the shadow of death. You have encountered this place of powerful metaphor by descending to the depths to meet your wounded soul at its most vulnerable. Slowly you have made your way to the other side. At last you have made your way through grief, your personal valley of the shadow of death.

Prayer: God, you have guided my way through the valley of the shadow of death. Though I have not always been as fearless as the psalmist, I am grateful for the protection and comfort of your care. Amen.

Assurance: **I see now that acceptance is on the spiritual side of the valley of the shadow of death.**

Day 2

The LORD is my shepherd, I shall not want.
Psalm 23:1 RSV

Thought: The experience of grief is often referred to as a journey. A journey is usually longer and more difficult than a short trip. When it begins, you do not know the destination of your grief journey. Have you ever set out on a trip without some idea of where you were going, the best way to get there, or when you would arrive? The unknown path of your journey through the valley of the shadow of death makes the quest for spiritual acceptance of death a formidable challenge.

Prayer: God, you are my shepherd. Along the journey I have been through the valley of the shadow of death and have found your presence at every turn. In acceptance you show me the way back to life. Amen.

Assurance: **My grief is a first-person journey.**

Day 3

He makes me lie down in green pastures. He leads me beside still waters.
Psalm 23:2 RSV

Thought: On the journey through grief there are, at first, only occasional green pastures until one day the landscape of the valley of the shadow of death becomes a vast expanse of beauty and wonder. Along the way you experience moments beside still waters that refresh and animate your soul. Those who have walked the road of grief before you have left behind a well-worn path that leads to greener pastures of life. Their testimony of stamina and fortitude strengthens your resolve to accept the peace that is beside still waters.

Prayer: God, along the journey of grief you have, indeed, made me lie down from time to time to enjoy your oases of quiet and rest. Thank you for insisting that I rest with you beside still waters. Amen.

Assurance: **My place of "still waters"—a glassy lake, a seaside retreat, a reflecting pool, a burbling fountain—can be anywhere there is peace.**

Day 4

He leads me in paths of righteousness for his name's sake.
Psalm 23:3b RSV

Thought: Through the blind uncertainty of grief, you have crossed and now ascend from the valley of the shadow of death. Your journey through grief has been one of slow, laborious footwork. "Even though I walk . . ." (Psalm 23:4 NIV). You were not asked to jog, run, or race but to walk. You put one foot in front of the other, sometimes only one half-step at a time. But your direction has always been forward on the road to acceptance through the valley of the shadow of death.

Prayer: God, for your name's sake I have traveled this rough, lonely road of grief. I look forward now to paths of righteousness in your abundant life ahead. Amen.

Assurance: **I walk forward through grief in paths of righteousness.**

Day 5

Surely goodness and mercy shall follow me all the days of my life;
and I shall dwell in the house of the LORD for ever.
Psalm 23:6 RSV

Thought: Your journey through grief is nuanced by the contrasts of light and dark, which create shadow. With acceptance, you recognize this as the long shadow cast by death, a shadow that both precedes and follows. "Even though I walk through the valley of the shadow of death . . ." (Psalm 23:4 RSV). Inherent within shadow is the suggestion of light. Without light there can be no shadow. You have made your way through the valley of the shadow of death because of light hidden within the shadow. You have persevered through grief because, at the end of the journey, yours is the promise of light in acceptance.

Prayer: God, through shadow you have followed me with your goodness and mercy. I am grateful that when the days of my life are past I will dwell in your house forever. Amen.

Assurance: **The light of God's goodness and mercy dwells within each shadow.**

Day 6

He restores my soul.
Psalm 23:3a RSV

Thought: Grief is not, as many would say, time that has done its work; rather, you do the work of grief to the point of mental, physical, emotional, and spiritual exhaustion. That is why it is vital to pause and rest on the journey through grief. Unexpected setbacks, detours, and side trips of illness or infirmity happen along the way. Your emotional ups and downs keep you on the uneven pavement of a bumpy road. Your interactions with those who do not understand your grief isolate you on the rough shoulders of a narrow, less-traveled highway. Acceptance is about spiritual restoration on the off-ramp of the journey through grief.

Prayer: God, you ask me to stop and rest on the journey for the refreshment of your restorative love. Thank you for your faithful guidance through the valley of the shadow of death on my way toward acceptance. Amen.

Assurance: **Without rest there can be no restoration.**

Day 7 – Rest for Your Soul

But those who wait for the LORD shall renew their strength,
they shall mount up with wings like eagles.
Isaiah 40:31 NRSV

Thought: When you wait for the Lord, in time your strength will be renewed. Think about an eagle soaring through the sky, its wings outstretched. An eagle can fly high, soar continually, and stay higher longer than other birds because its wings have great lifting power. In grief, God provides the lifting power. As you accept and soar, God renews your strength.

Prayer: God, in acceptance, I long for renewed strength. As I rest my soul from grief today, I pray for the lifting power of your grace so that I may again soar in life. Amen.

Assurance: **God gives me lifting power to soar with wings like an eagle— upward toward God.**

Perspective

Return, O my soul, to your rest,
for the LORD has dealt bountifully with you.
Psalm 116:7 NRSV

Thought: In grief, the order of life becomes the randomness of reinventing life without your loved one. Perhaps for a while you feel like the reluctant resident of a deserted, unfamiliar island—a strange place, unfriendly to its habitation by your soul and spirit on the journey through grief. Acceptance is moving beyond the turmoil and total upheaval of death to a life reordered in peace. Stand, at last renewed and made whole in the assurance that there is life in acceptance because there is life after death.

Prayer: God, you have moved me from the pain and sorrow of grief toward acceptance and new life. I give thanks that you have dealt bountifully with me. My mind reawakens to life, my body is at rest, my heart contemplates joy, and my soul abides in you forever. Amen.

Assurance: **My acceptance is the doorway to new life.**

Grief Is Acceptance

GRIEF IS HOPE

From time to time when situations required perspective, Leighton would say, "No one has cancer, and no one has died." This was his description of life's worst eventualities. In ninety short, yet very long days, we experienced both. The very intimation of cancer gripped my entire being. The illness took over his life, my life, and our life together. It became our life. I tried with all my human might to encounter and defeat the enemy. It could not be conquered by mere mortal will. I soldiered on, and through the battle I functioned and existed despite the certainty of imminent death. For me it was death witnessed on collision course. Cancer, the disease that invaded and ended his life, was greater than us both.

The dread of pain roiled Leighton's spirit and taunted his waning body. We assimilated the facts as we understood them. We talked not in realities but in practicalities. We were guarded in our optimism and superficially hopeful with each other. Our solidarity was a silent force that required no words. We knew what was likely ahead, but we did not confront the worst. There was never that white-knuckle conversation when we might have called the disease by its name, wept, and railed against the inequity that threatened our very mortality as husband and wife.

The reality of death is so harsh. Intellectually, I knew that he would die. He had terminal cancer. Emotionally, I hoped that he would recover, even until the last minute, the last second of his life. It is, in fact, the very nature of the human heart to hope, to believe in our own immortality and in the idea that somehow we will never die.

From the abyss of hopelessness I wondered whether there would ever be more to my life than just death. I questioned whether there was yet life ahead, a reason to look forward, to hope. The daily struggle between my head and heart was to look heavenward rather than to the grave, to trust that there is hope and a future through the grace of God. I know that I am ready to cross the threshold toward the future that God has planned for me. The past was real, but it will never be the present again. I remember and long for what was, yet I know that life is today. This is the present, the only moment that is now. I hope.

Preparation

For God alone my soul waits in silence,
for my hope is from him.
Psalm 62:5 NRSV

Thought: Grief leads to hope. One day you find yourself there. There are a few questions yet unresolved, but you are making your way down the road on the journey through grief. You look ahead, eager to move forward out of grief and back into the mainstream of life. You believe that there is a future; you discern at last that for which you should hope. You pray for strength to be in the world because you are changed and curiously fortified by the experience of grief. Grief can be the most honest and faithful place you stand to find hope.

Prayer: God, my hope is from you alone. My soul waits for you in silence, ready to receive the gift of hope. Amen.

Assurance: **The light of hope is my strength, my joy, and my peace.**

Week 1 – Healing

Day 1

He heals the brokenhearted
and binds up their wounds.
Psalm 147:3 NRSV

Thought: Healing and wholeness are for those willing to be vulnerable enough to be made strong. The question of hope is whether you will entertain the possibility of being healed from grief or will prefer to live with a permanently broken heart. You may ask, "Is there healing from grief?" Perhaps you wonder how long it will take you to heal from grief—or even if you will heal. There is healing from grief.

Prayer: God, I hope in the assurance that you are healing my broken heart. You bind up my wounds with your love and grace. May I hope in you. Amen.

Assurance: **I imagine myself healed from grief.**

Day 2

Then your light will break forth like the dawn, and your healing will quickly appear;then your righteousness will go before you, and the glory of the LORD will be your rear guard.Then you will call, and the LORD will answer; you will cry for help, and he will say: Here am I.
Isaiah 58:8-9 NIV

Thought: The best analogy for healing in grief is the human body. When you have a physical injury, it causes a finite wound. In most cases the damage is reparable; the wound is treated with the expectation of healing. Death wounds your human soul and spirit; it causes you to grieve. For some, the wound is immeasurable— so deep that healing seems impossible. For others, the wound is less severe. Like any physical injury, the wound of grief must be taken seriously. Honest, accurate assessment facilitates its treatment, both mentally and spiritually. Most wounds of the body can be healed. All wounds of the soul can be healed.

Prayer: God, I wait for your light in the expectation of healing. In grief, my cry has been to you for help. In healing, I hear your voice, "Here am I." Amen.

Assurance: **The larger my wound, the deeper my love for the one I have lost.**

Day 3

One who is often reproved, yet remains stubborn, will suddenly be broken beyond healing.
Proverbs 29:1 NRSV

Thought: In your moments of acute woundedness, you may resist healing from grief with uncharacteristic but willful stubbornness. You may think that you are broken beyond healing, that you never will be whole again. If this is your personal assessment, you may try to anesthetize your pain with easy remedies. Likely you have found that this does not work. Quick cures seldom last. God is the one true source of reconstructive relief from the pain of your grief on the way to healing.

Prayer: God, there are moments when I stubbornly resist healing. Yet I want to live again beyond the broken heart. Reprove my spirit until it complies with yours. Amen.

Assurance: **There is no timeline or prescribed cure date for grief.**

Day 4

I mourn, and horror grips me. Is there no balm in Gilead?
Is there no physician there? Why then is there
no healing for the wound of my people?
Jeremiah 8:21-22 NIV

Thought: Relentless, unremitting grief is like an infection; it invades the wound of your soul and stubbornly resists treatment. When grief permanently overwhelms you, it can destroy your very will to live. If your grief is tenacious, spiritual healing begins when you affirm, at last, that you want to be made well. You want your journey through grief to be over.

Prayer: God, you are the balm in Gilead; you are the great physician. Heal the wounds of my soul. I want to be made well. Amen.

Assurance: **My healing is the gradual process of becoming whole.**

Day 5

"I will heal my people and will let them enjoy
abundant peace and security."
Jeremiah 33:6 NIV

Thought: When you are injured, wound dressings are carefully applied to your physical body to promote healing and protect the point of invasion from germs. Similarly, in grief you may slap a figurative bandage on your wound, not so much to promote healing but to protect yourself from additional hurt and pain. Because you may sense that others do not want to see the gaping hole in your spirit—the imperfect part of your life that is grief—you cover it up using your own self-styled emotional first aid. When you at last take off your protective bandage and find that you are well, you see that you are healed both inside and out.

Prayer: God, I trust in your promise of healing. Thank you for the hope of your abundant peace in the security of your love. Amen.

Assurance: **There will be a faint scar forever in my soul to remind me of my grief.**

Day 6

*Those troubled by impure spirits were cured, and the
people all tried to touch him, because
power was coming from him
and healing them all.*
Luke 6:18-19 NIV

Thought: Spiritual and emotional healing from grief is perhaps best described as recovery. You convalesce for a while and recuperate from grief. Then you turn a corner and forge ahead into life. If you are finding satisfaction again in life, then you are recovering. Likely you have heard yourself say, whether silently or aloud, "I am better," "I want to live," "Life is good," or some other self-talk that is affirmative and positive. This is a sure indication that you are recovering from grief.

Prayer: God, I rest in the power of Christ. His healing and hope come to me as a gift of your Holy Spirit. Amen.

Assurance: **The spiritual and emotional remnant of my most acute pain is my scar, now part of who I am.**

Day 7 – Rest for Your Soul

*He welcomed them and spoke to them about
the kingdom of God, and healed those
who needed healing.*
Luke 9:11 NIV

Thought: It is a medical fact that scar tissue becomes the strongest part of your body. As your spirit slowly heals from grief, you become strongest in your broken places—within the very fiber of your soul. Though for a while you are wounded by the death of your loved one, your broken heart one day is healed by God's triumphant adequacy.

Prayer: God, on this day of rest for my soul, I am living proof of your power to heal. You welcome me this day to new hope in the promise of your eternal kingdom. I am grateful for your divine healing. Amen.

Assurance: **My scar affirms the best part of my own immortality: my soul.**

Week 2 – Confidence

Day 1

"The LORD is my portion" says my soul, "therefore I will hope in him."
The LORD is good to those who wait for him, to the soul that seeks him.
It is good that one should wait quietly for the salvation of the LORD.
Lamentations 3:24-26 NRSV

Thought: On some level, the death of your loved one perhaps has imperiled your self-confidence. Hope engenders confidence as you master the realities of daily life. Your confidence, once lost to grief, returns as you learn new modalities of independence. It is no longer dismal to eat alone; you are comfortable in your own company. You provide for yourself; there is satisfaction in business management or earning a living. You care for yourself; you pay attention to your medical needs and honor your body. Confidence surges when your life is more about hope than about grief.

Prayer: God, from the depths of a grateful heart I hope in you. You renew my confidence in life with your goodness. My soul seeks you. I wait for you. Amen.

Assurance: **In hope my spirit wants to "start fresh."**

Day 2

Be strong and take heart, all you who hope in the LORD.
Psalm 31:24 NIV

Thought: The seesaw of grief and hope teeters between two choices: living in apathy born of fatalism or living in passion born of hope. A sense of fatalism due to the death of your loved one tempts you to live in smallness rather than fullness, a kind of lifeless nothingness that feeds fatalism and obscures the hope of any passion yet to be. Even as you move forward with hope into life, grief may compel you from time to time to sift back through the events of life for unmined treasure to store up in your heart. These are the memories of hope. This is the promise of passion yet to be.

Prayer: God, may the hope that comes from and abides in you strengthen me to live in passion born of hope. Amen.

Assurance: **In hope my newborn life begins—passions reawakening.**

Day 3

May the God of hope fill you with all joy and peace in believing, so that you may abound in hope by the power of the Holy Spirit.
Romans 15:13 NRSV

Thought: How do you rebuild confidence after the death of your loved one? You do not do it entirely alone but with the support of community. At work, in your church, or in your volunteer service you experience restored confidence as you engage and take on new duties or responsibilities. Your self-confidence is bolstered by the satisfaction of a hobby or recreation. You are affirmed by the enrichment and enjoyment of independent travel. Your children, grandchildren, and friends assure you that you are of value to them and to others. Your confidence is renewed in the hope of life.

Prayer: God, there is joy and peace in believing in you and your plan for my life. Help me to not only hope but also abound in hope. Amen.

Assurance: **My hope in grief is my confidence in the divine plan of the loving, caring God who is the author of all hope.**

Day 4

Why are you cast down, O my soul,
and why are you disquieted within me?
Hope in God; for I shall again praise him,
my help and my God.
Psalm 43:5 NRSV

Thought: In hope you may yet experience a silent, inner struggle to move from the defensiveness of grief to the quiet confidence of living forward. It is difficult to imagine or even reckon with the moment when the worst of grief is over and behind you—when every breath is no longer one of sorrow for your loved one. You reach the other side of the valley of the shadow of death when grief as an embedded, familiar mode of thinking and being slowly begins to feel stiff and stifling.

Prayer: God, there are moments when I am easily downcast, still disturbed by death and grief. I hope in your help and praise you, my God. Amen.

Assurance: **In the will to hope I find the strength to live and the courage to die.**

Day 5

Hope does not disappoint us, because God's love has been poured into our hearts through the Holy Spirit that has been given to us.
Romans 5:5 NRSV

Thought: Because of God's love, "hope does not disappoint." Yet in the worst moments of grief, it feels almost impossible to hope. Those are the times you may ask, "Where is God's love?" The message of hope echoes in your heart yet seems dissonant with the reality of life. Grief is the disappointment of unfulfilled dreams and plans. Hope is the ongoing nurture of fortitude and faithfulness.

Prayer: God, you pour your love into my heart through the Holy Spirit in the assurance that hope will never disappoint. Thank you for the wonder and promise of hope. Amen.

Assurance: **Hope is my disappointment defeated.**

Day 6

In quietness and confidence shall be your strength.
Isaiah 30:15 NKJV

Thought: The relearning of self-confidence occurs in a kind of post-grief puberty—the moment that lies somewhere between the waning sorrow of grief and newfound hope. This period of growth and instruction challenges you to rediscover yourself as a person of individual value and worth. Yet this moment in life may feel tepid and lukewarm. There is neither the cold darkness of grief nor the warm light of hope. Rather, this is a quiet phase, a time of readying, resting, and regrouping after the long journey through grief. It is a time of active waiting. Breathe, relax, rest. Learn again to hope.

Prayer: God, thank you for quiet moments to grow in confidence and in your strength. Amen.

Assurance: **I stretch toward the open road of life—the way of hope, surprise, and joy.**

Day 7 – Rest for Your Soul

And you will have confidence, because there is hope;
you will be protected and take your rest in safety.
Job 11:18 NRSV

Thought: Hope is more than an emotion. Hope is more than naïve optimism or wishful thinking. Hope is more than a positive attitude. Hope is more than a passive wish or dream. On this day of rest for your soul, abide in the safety of authentic spiritual hope.

Prayer: God, I have confidence because there is hope. May I rest this day in the protection of hope. Amen.

Assurance: **I hope for the future because the future belongs to God**.

Week 3 – Assurance

Day 1

My goal is that their hearts would be encouraged and united together in love, so that they might have all the riches of assurance that come with understanding, so that they might have the knowledge of the secret plan of God, namely Christ.
Colossians 2:2 CEB

Thought: Within grief is the assurance of eternal life through Christ. This is the one thing in all of grief that is absolute. You grieve the death of your loved one, yet you take comfort in the assurance that there is life after death, that death is transformation rather than termination. The meditations of the next days focus on the assurances of the Beatitudes. The riches of assurance in Christ come with understanding his words.

Prayer: God, encourage my heart in the riches of your assurance. May I be united with you in love to know your plan in Christ. Amen.

Assurance: **Understanding inspires my assurance.**

Day 2
"You're blessed when you're at the end of your rope. With less of you there is more of God and his rule."
Matthew 5:3 *THE MESSAGE*

Thought: Sometimes the word *blessed* is translated as "happy." Blessed is a state of inner joy and peace with a "soul happiness" that transcends the world. Christ's assurance of being blessed is the divine reward for perseverance through the trials of life. Grief is perhaps the greatest test of spiritual character that you will ever encounter. You know what it feels like to be at the end of your rope. The assurance is that when you are humbled by your own limitations, the resources of God are inexhaustible.

Prayer: God, when I come to the end of my rope, you teach me to tie a knot and hang on. May there be less of me and more of you in my daily walk toward the end of grief. Amen.

Assurance: **Blessed is a spiritual state; it is an attitude of grace.**

Day 3

"You're blessed when you're content with just who you are—no more, no less.
That's the moment you find yourselves proud owners of
everything that can't be bought."
Matthew 5:5 *THE MESSAGE*

Thought: On the journey through grief, gradually you become reacquainted with yourself. You learn how to function without your loved one. Slowly you individuate. You see yourself for who you are, emotionally and spiritually. You learn more about confidence and self-affirmation. Introspection speaks to you of both weakness and strength. Perhaps you like the person you discover yourself to be and are content with who you are.

Prayer: God, I am grateful for accessible words of assurance. Through your grace I am the proud owner of everything that can't be bought. Amen.

Assurance: **If I am content with who I am, I have done the work of grief.**

Day 4

"You're blessed when you've worked up a good
appetite for God. He's food and drink
in the best meal you'll ever eat."
Matthew 5:6 *THE MESSAGE*

Thought: Near the end of grief likely you experience a thirst to be refilled by the adventure of life. You are hungry to rediscover vitality after the long journey of grief. You have worked up a good appetite for life and renewal in God. There is no better feast.

Prayer: God, you alone satisfy my hungry heart. I am grateful for the bounty of your love at the table of your grace. Amen.

Assurance: **God is the food and drink of the best meal I will ever eat.**

Day 5

"You're blessed when you care.
At the moment of being 'care-full,'
you find yourselves cared for."
Matthew 5:7 *THE MESSAGE*

Thought: On the long journey through the valley of the shadow of death, you have experienced many variations on the theme of care. There were perhaps moments when you did not care about anyone or anything except the searing pain of sorrow. There were times when it was easier to be apathetic than to care about life and the future. Yet throughout the seasons of grief, you were enfolded by the care of others and, above all else, by the care of God. Now is the moment to be care-full. "Freely you have received, freely give" (Matthew 10:8 NIV).

Prayer: God, thank you that my heart is ready and able to care again. You have blessed me with your faithful care. May I give the gift of care in your name to others. Amen.

Assurance: **I am filled with care in grateful response to the care I have received in grief.**

Day 6

"You're blessed when you get your
inside world—your mind and heart—put right.
Then you can see God in the outside world."
Matthew 5:8 *THE MESSAGE*

Thought: Grief is, in part, about sorting out and reassembling your inside world after the death of your loved one. At the moment you feel present to yourself again—changed yet returned after a long and precarious absence from the world—you respond to the irresistible emotional urge to engage and venture forth again. Perhaps you reach out to encounter a stranger for even a moment, testing to see if there still is a heart within you that validates the mechanics of a long-unused smile. When your mind and heart are restored to full citizenship within yourself, you see clear evidence of God in the outside world.

Prayer: God, through the nurture of the Holy Spirit you have restored my inside world. I am grateful that my mind and heart are again attuned to life so that I better see you at work in the world. Amen.

Assurance: **Grief is about the realignment of my mind and heart.**

Day 7 – Rest for Your Soul

"You're blessed when you can show people how to cooperate instead of compete or fight. That's when you discover who you really are, and your place in God's family."
Matthew 5:9 THE MESSAGE

Thought: Your newfound sense of what is really important in life is a priceless gift of grief. The hard-won perspective of grief allows you to build a bridge for others into the way of peace and light. "You're blessed when you feel you've lost what is most dear to you. Only then can you be embraced by the One most dear to you" (Matthew 5:4 *THE MESSAGE*).

Prayer: God, on this day of rest for my soul, I am grateful that I have a place in your family. May I rest in you this day and always. Amen.

Assurance: **When I invest myself in others and in life, I discover who I really am.**

Week 4 – God's Faithfulness

Day 1

The steadfast love of the LORD never ceases, his mercies never come to an end; they are new every morning; great is your faithfulness.
Lamentations 3:22-23 NRSV

Thought: God uses grief to teach you more of God's faithfulness. When at last you slowly awaken from the coma-like state of grief, you perhaps experience a moment of divine understanding about the faithfulness of God. In that moment your eyes and heart are opened to these eternal truths: God is ageless. God is timeless. God is unchanging. God is for all generations. God is from everlasting to everlasting. God is eternal. God is faithful.

Prayer: God, I stand before you in awe and wonder as I awaken each day to your new mercies. I am grateful for your endless faithfulness to me. Amen.

Assurance: **The faithfulness of God endures forever.**

Day 2

I have loved you with an everlasting love; therefore I have continued my faithfulness to you.
Jeremiah 31:3 NRSV

Thought: Faithfulness is the power of everlasting love. Faithfulness is the pledge of marriage for a life built together to last forever, "until death do us part." Faithfulness is the absolute nature of God. You emerge from the spiritual and emotional isolation of grief when you realize with absolute certainty that God is faithful.

Prayer: God, your faithfulness has saved my life. Through my grief you have continued to hear and answer the cries of my heart. I am grateful for your everlasting love. Amen.

Assurance: **God's faithfulness is beyond all thought or human imagination.**

Day 3

Do not, O Lord, withhold your mercy from me;
let your steadfast love and your faithfulness keep me safe for ever.
Psalm 40:11 NRSV

Thought: When you attune your inmost heart to the gifts of grief, you discern with gratitude every manifestation of God's faithfulness. God is faithful; God continuously protects you. God watches over you, especially if you live alone—perhaps for the first time in life. God is faithful; God gives you an extra measure of strength and forbearance. You ask yourself in amazement, "How did I do that?" "Did I really accomplish that?" The faithfulness of God blesses you and keeps you safe forever.

Prayer: God, though I have wandered through grief at times apart from you, you have never withheld your mercy from me. Thank you for the spiritual haven of safety in your abiding faithfulness. Amen.

Assurance: **I am safe in the faithfulness of God.**

Day 4

O Lord, you are my God; I will exalt you and praise your name,
for in perfect faithfulness you have done marvelous things,
things planned long ago.
Isaiah 25:1 NIV

Thought: Near the end of the journey through grief, take time for spiritual reflection on the faithfulness of God as your life has grown and changed through grief. How has God's faithfulness manifested to you? Have you experienced moments of awakening to the reality of God faithfulness? In what ways? Is there personal evidence of God's faithfulness that you recognize and cherish? Perspective requires reflection to exalt and praise.

Prayer: God, in perfect faithfulness you have walked every step with me on the journey through grief. O Lord, you are my God. Amen.

Assurance: **I hope for those marvelous things planned for me long ago.**

Day 5

Your steadfast love, O LORD, extends to the heavens,
your faithfulness to the clouds.
Psalm 36:5 NRSV

Thought: What do you see when you look at the sky? If it is a clear night, there are stars or perhaps the soft glow of moonlight. By day, clouds expand and shift across the visible horizon as far as the eye can see. Our spiritual vision is also our human limitation. It is, in fact, impossible to see or even imagine love and faithfulness as endless and vast as heaven except in faith.

Prayer: God, when I see the beauty of clouds I am reminded of your faithfulness. Thank you for the vast expanse of your love. Amen.

Assurance: **I see the faithfulness of God in the beauty of all creation.**

Day 6

Give thanks to him, bless his name. For the LORD is good; his steadfast love
endures forever, and his faithfulness to all generations.
Psalm 100:4-5 NRSV

Thought: God is faithful to all generations. God has been there to comfort all who have grieved throughout the ages of time. God is with all who now grieve. God will be faithful to those you love who yet will grieve. You assure others of God's faithfulness in the reflection of your spiritual maturity as a survivor. You have grieved and, at last, conquered grief through the power of God's faithfulness.

Prayer: God, I give you thanks and bless your name for your goodness and faithfulness to me in grief. Amen.

Assurance: **My experience of grief bears witness to the faithfulness of God.**

Day 7 – Rest for Your Soul

*Know therefore that the LORD your God is God; he is the faithful God, keeping
his covenant of love to a thousand generations of those who love
Him and keep his commands.*
Deuteronomy 7:9 NIV

Thought: On this day of rest for your soul, contemplate the historic certainty of God's faithfulness to a thousand generations of those who love God. It is inconceivable to imagine the thousand generations that contemplate the infinite nature of God's love. Be faithful; receive God's faithfulness.

Prayer: God, I rest this day in your covenant of love and faithfulness. You are the Lord, my God. You are God. Amen.

Assurance: **God is faithful; I will keep God's commands.**

Perspective

*Now hope that is seen is not hope. For who hopes for what is seen? But if we
hope for what we do not see, we wait for it with patience.*
Romans 8:24-25 NRSV

Thought: Hope is invisible. It is more than an aspiration or a heartfelt desire. Hope is born of your spirit enlivened by faith. You cannot see hope, but you know what it feels like to hope. Without hope, life is bland and uninspired. Hope is the salt of life that flavors; it is the seasoning that adds spice to your expectation of life. "For who hopes for what is seen?" Hope in God.

Prayer: God, you teach me to hope through healing. You lift my heart in confidence for the future. You inspire my hope with assurance. You empower my life with your faithfulness. I give you thanks that I again hope. Amen.

Assurance: **I hope for what is unseen and wait for it with patience.**

Grief Is Hope

_____

_____

_____

_____

_____

_____

_____

_____

_____

_____

_____

_____

_____

_____

_____

_____

_____

_____

GRIEF IS TRUST

Leighton trusted me implicitly. When he got sick, he relied on my strength and self-sufficiency for his physical and emotional support. In fact, I felt woefully inadequate to the daunting task of his daily care. We discussed getting a second opinion before his hospitalization; he decided to continue with the doctors who were treating him. I felt that it was not appropriate for me to try to dissuade him or preempt his right to make his own healthcare decisions for as long as he was able or willing to do so. On the day he entered the hospital, never again to leave, at last he was relieved to give over the decision making to someone else—to me. He knew that my complete devotion and deep, abiding love would never fail when all else seemed so lost. He entrusted to me the decisions of his care—even his very life.

After the relentless downward spiral of the last, long weekend, around midnight on Sunday I said the words "no more" firmly, spontaneously, and instinctively. These were the most difficult words I have ever spoken. I knew the time had come to honor Leighton's end of life directives—to do that which he wanted for himself—and, as his trustee, to act in his sole best interest. He trusted me to advocate and, if necessary, to make this heartbreaking decision on his behalf. Leighton did not want his life prolonged with no hope of recovery. It was the greater part of love to give him up and let him go. It was time. This is doubtless the very hardest thing that I have ever done in my life, or that I will ever do. He honored me with his trust.

Preparation

Surely God is my salvation; I will trust, and will not be afraid, for the LORD GOD is my strength and my might; he has become my salvation.
Isaiah 12:2 NRSV

Thought: Grief is trust. Trust and fear are at opposite ends of the spectrum of human emotion. In grief it becomes almost a reflex to succumb to fear rather than live in bold declaration of trust. What God expects of you is trust, especially as you grieve. Even when you cannot fully comprehend where life has been or where it is leading, you respond to God in grief with a love that dares to trust.

Prayer: God, you offer me the might of your saving grace. As I learn again to trust, may I renounce the fear of grief and live in your strength. Amen.

Assurance: **In grief I am learning the meaning of absolute trust.**

Week 1 – God's Plan

Day 1

Trust in the LORD with all your heart...
Proverbs 3:5a NRSV

Thought: You know what it is to say to your loved one, "I love you with all of my heart." The words echo in your heart from that time in life when they expressed the love of your relationship. You know what it is to love with all of your heart. Yet you may find it difficult to trust with all of your heart. Because of the pain of grief, you may be reluctant to entrust to God all of your heart—all of your broken heart. No closed corners, no unopened doors, no reservations. Not half-hearted, but wholehearted trust. Trust with all of your heart.

Prayer: God, you ask me to trust you with all of my heart. In grief it feels easier to love you than to trust you, yet your grace proves that it is impossible to love without trust. May I trust you with all of my broken heart. Amen.

Assurance: **I know that my heart is large and loving without the mantle of grief.**

Day 2
...and do not rely on your own insight.
Proverbs 3:5b NRSV

Thought: A challenge of grief is the notion that there is any insight other than your own. Yet the one certainty about your own insight is that it is limited. It has no farther span than the imagination of your own mind. God's insight is limitless. It is infinite. When your spirit is impoverished by grief, you perhaps feel for a while that you can trust only that of which you are sure—your own resources. Yet likely you experience time and again how unreliable your own resources actually are. Do you rely on your insight or trust the insight of God?

Prayer: God, you have given me the ability to think and imagine, yet I understand that my insight and resources are limited. Help me as I struggle with self-reliance instead of complete trust in you. Amen.

Assurance: **In grief I better understand the difference between reliance and trust.**

Day 3

For now we see in a mirror, dimly, but then we will see face to face.
1 Corinthians 13:12 NRSV

Thought: God explains the mystery of trust using the imagery of a mirror. Although the surface of a mirror is reflective, it is opaque rather than transparent. What you see when you look into the mirror is no more and no less than yourself. There is no deeper image beyond or through the looking glass. In God's all-wise, all-knowing, and all-seeing plan, God alone knows how your life fits into the larger plan of creation. Until the dimly reflected mirror image of life is illuminated by the full light of eternity, you abide in the mystery of trust.

Prayer: God, I long to know your plan and understand fully the mystery of life and death. I am grateful that in Christ I will one day see you face to face. Until then I trust in you. Amen.

Assurance: **The nature of my heart is to love and trust.**

Day 4

All this also comes from the LORD Almighty, whose plan is wonderful, whose wisdom is magnificent.
Isaiah 28:29 NIV

Thought: When you are wounded, you are vulnerable. When you are vulnerable, you are sometimes unwilling to trust, even God. Perhaps especially God. The heart in conflict because of grief is an onlooker to trust. A wonderful plan born of God's infinite wisdom seems almost unimaginable. This is the doorway of trust that opens to the rest of your life.

Prayer: God, I am vulnerable and wounded by the death of my loved one. At times it is so difficult to trust. I pray that I may encounter your magnificent wisdom, even in grief. Amen.

Assurance: **I trust God's wonderful plan for my life.**

Day 5

And those who know your name put their trust in you,
for you, O LORD, have not forsaken those who seek you.
Psalm 9:10 NRSV

Thought: On the upward bound ascent of the journey through grief, it is important to stay in step with God rather than anticipate God's plan. When you walk forward in trust, you may feel for a while as though you are constantly lagging behind, grasping for God's outstretched hand ahead. There are moments of renewed self-reliance along the way when you want to take charge rather than trust in God, walking patiently hand in hand. If you get ahead of God's plan, you miss the moment of perfect trust in God's perfect plan executed in perfect timing for your life ahead.

Prayer: God, because of your unfailing faithfulness to me through the dark days of grief, I seek you with greater trust than ever before in my life. I am grateful that you have never forsaken me. I know your name and put my trust in you. Amen.

Assurance: **There is no greater trust than to walk hand in hand with God.**

Day 6

I am God, and there is no other;
I am God, and there is no one like me,
declaring the end from the beginning
and from ancient times things not yet done,
saying, "My purpose shall stand,
and I will fulfill my intention"
. . . .
I have spoken, and I will bring it to pass;
I have planned, and I will do it.
Isaiah 46:9-11 NRSV

Thought: The power of historical perspective in the infinite nature of God inspires trust, especially in grief. God proves in the order of the universe alone that God's plan is intentional. God is neither haphazard nor random in the design and purpose for all of life, most especially for your life. There is no other God; there is no one like God. God alone knows the beginning and end and the unique plan for you. Does the experience of death and grief inspire your trust in God?

Prayer: God, I am in awe of your powerful plan for all of life forever. I believe that you will fulfill your intention for my life and that you have a plan that will be done. Amen.

Assurance: **God speaks; I listen in trust to God's plan for my life.**

Day 7 – Rest for Your Soul

As I have designed,
so shall it be;
and as I have planned,
so shall it come to pass.
Isaiah 14:24 NRSV

Thought: As with any viable plan, there is an architect who designs the structure and executes the details so that the end result reflects the plan. On this day of rest for your soul, trust in God's plan. You are designed to perfection by the master architect whose plan for your life will come to pass.

Prayer: God, when I step away from the remains of grief I have a better view of your plan. I will never understand death, but I trust that, in a way yet unknown to me, grief is part of your plan for my life in you. Amen.

Assurance: **I believe that the plan designed by God especially for my life will come to pass.**

Week 2 – Others

Day 1

Our heart is glad in him,
because we trust in his holy name.
Psalm 33:21 NRSV

Thought: With the death of your loved one, it may feel as though your whole world has been turned upside down and inside out. A serious side effect of loss is that, for a while, trust seems compromised. You may feel irrationally betrayed by the inability of medical professionals who could not save the life of your loved one. Perhaps you feel that you cannot trust those who offer care and perspective. When death shatters your world, trust in others may be a momentary casualty. It is a normal part of grief to retreat and withhold trust for a while.

Prayer: God, trust in others is a formidable challenge. I pray that you will conform my wounded spirit to accept the human limitations of others and of myself. Amen.

Assurance: **In unconditional trust there is gladness of heart.**

Day 2

Trust in the LORD, and do good;
so you will live in the land, and enjoy security.
Psalm 37:3 NRSV

Thought: Whom do you trust with your emotional vulnerability in grief? The intimacy required to share your grief with another demands unreserved trust. Someone of depth, compassion, or personal experience whom you trust will allow you to talk and pour out your heart without judgment or easy, formulaic advice. Perhaps you neither need nor want professional counseling or therapy—only the listening ear of a confidential friend. In grief it takes inordinate trust to believe that you can be truly heard, understood, or comforted by another human being.

Prayer: God, I desire the security of complete trust in you. May I learn again to open my heart to the listening care of others. Amen.

Assurance: **When I listen in love, I do something good for someone else.**

Day 3

Commit your way to the LORD;
trust in him, and he will act.
Psalm 37:5 NRSV

Thought: When grief overwhelms the daily landscape of your life, your innate sense of trust is tested as well-meaning friends or family offer clichés and platitudes to assuage the pain of your loss. Unless another has experienced personal loss, declarations such as "I understand," "I know how you feel," or "I know exactly how you feel" resound as empty words that likely hurt more than help. A component of trust is authenticity. Words that overlay grief's pain belie the intimacy of trust. In grief you trust the outreach of others, whatever words are used.

Prayer: God, may I be single-minded in my commitment to your way, especially as I grieve. When my trust is challenged, may I trust in you to act. Amen.

Assurance: **No one knows how I feel except me.**

Day 4

He put a new song in my mouth,
a song of praise to our God.
Many will see and fear,
and put their trust in the LORD.
Psalm 40:3 NRSV

Thought: It is a duty of grief to learn the fine art of dismissing the sometimes thoughtless comments of others. Pronouncements meant to console you are often presumptions that trivialize grief: "It's for the best," "Everyone dies sooner or later," "She's not suffering anymore," "He's better off." You are hurt and upset when careless comments add to the indignities of grief. You may feel that those who fail to understand your grief cannot be entrusted with the pain of your heart. Forgive and forget those words that hurt your heart.

Prayer: God, as grief subsides and my spiritual perspective improves, I better understand the words of others. May the experience of grief enlarge my heart to unrestrained trust. Amen.

Assurance: **My new song is of praise and trust.**

Day 5

Blessed are those who trust in the LORD,
whose trust is the LORD.
Jeremiah 17:7 NRSV

Thought: Sharing your story within the sanctity of a group of people who know the experience of death and grief may assure you that are not alone in your loss. In a safe community of mutual trust, you find support and encouragement as you seek a life of renewed hope and joy after your personal experience of grief. When others who understand extend the lifeline of trust, you are certain that you are heard and understood.

Prayer: God, you are the source and resource of all trust. You are my trust. Amen.

Assurance: **I will share with others who understand the sacred bond of trust in grief.**

Day 6

*Many will see and fear
and put their trust in the* LORD.
Psalm 40:3 NRSV

Thought: The question remains: How do you restore trust in those you feel have been perhaps less than emotionally trustworthy through your grief? As humans, we are all imperfect. We say things better left unsaid; we blurt out words we later regret saying. Because of your acute emotional need for authentic understanding, your sensitivity to the imperfections of others is heightened by grief. The door is opened when you release the real or imagined offenses of others and live forward in renewed trust.

Prayer: God, I am coming through the dark valley of grief. I am grateful that fear has not imperiled my trust in you. Amen.

Assurance: **The fear of grief is overpowered by trust.**

Day 7 – Rest for Your Soul

O LORD *of hosts,
happy is everyone who trusts in you.*
Psalm 84:12 NRSV

Thought: On this day of rest for your soul, consider the blessing of trust. In trust you do not bear the burden of grief or life alone. Trust in the goodness and integrity of others. Trust that others love and care about you. Trust in the humanity of others. Allow for the humanness of others. Trust in God.

Prayer: God, there is a glimmer of happiness dawning in my life. I rest today in the blessing of complete trust in you, O Lord of hosts. Amen.

Assurance: **When I trust in God, I am blessed with even greater trust.**

Week 3 – Self

Day 1

The LORD *is my strength and my shield;
in him my heart trusts;*

> *so I am helped, and my heart exults,*
> *and with my song I give thanks to him.*
> Psalm 28:7 NRSV

Thought: One of the most unsettling effects of grief is the sense of a loss of trust in yourself. You may be unused to change; you may be uncomfortable with new demands on your physical and emotional resources that cause you to question yourself at every turn. You feel, perhaps, that you cannot trust your own decision-making abilities or that you are unable to care for yourself sufficiently. A loss of self-trust is a temporary state in grief.

Prayer: God, you are my shield. I am grateful for the help of your strength when I do not trust myself. In you my heart trusts. Amen.

Assurance: **God is trustworthy. I rejoice and give thanks.**

Day 2

> *But I trust in you, O LORD;*
> *I say, "You are my God."*
> Psalm 31:14 NRSV

Thought: In the aftermath of acute grief, you understand your sense of personal mistrust when you consider what trust really means. In grief trust means releasing fear. Trust means training your mind away from chronic anxiety. Trust means acknowledging that your understanding of life and death is the only thing in your life that certainly is insufficient. The rest is a matter of trust—in yourself and in God.

Prayer: God, I better understand the distinction between the personal mistrust of grief and the trust it takes to live in your sufficiency. You are my God. I trust in you. Amen.

Assurance: **As I release mistrust, I learn to trust again in myself.**

Day 3

> *For you, O LORD, are my hope,*
> *my trust, O LORD, from my youth.*
> Psalm 71:5 NRSV

Thought: In grief, you may be plagued by the sense that you cannot trust yourself enough to move forward in life. This is perhaps the moment for a serious accounting of your spiritual assets and liabilities. Likely the cause of your personal breakdown of trust is more imagined than real. God knows who you are, how you live, what is the span of your life, and what you may contribute while you yet have breath, whatever your circumstances. As God's beloved child, God's desire is for you to trust—in God and in yourself.

Prayer: God, you are present to me now as you have been every day of my life. May I return again to trust, for you are my hope and my trust. Amen.

Assurance: **My spiritual assets far outweigh the emotional liabilities of my grief.**

Day 4

Preserve my life, for I am devoted to you;
save your servant who trusts in you.
Psalm 86:2 NRSV

Thought: An aspect of personal mistrust is the issue of devotion. In relationship with your loved one, you loved with a complete devotion that forever will be a stronghold in your heart. The task of reconstructing self-trust is redirecting the devotion of your love. Devotion is giving to God in trust all of your heart. Devotion is the living presence of Christ at the center of your being. In devotion there is complete trust.

Prayer: God, I am your servant, even as I learn of trust again. I am grateful that you have preserved my life on the journey through grief. Amen.

Assurance: **There is devotion in my trust and trust in my devotion.**

Day 5

Therefore, let those suffering in accordance with God's will entrust themselves
to a faithful Creator, while continuing to do good.
1 Peter 4:19 NRSV

Thought: Grief is, indeed, suffering. Although it may be always difficult to reconcile death with God's will, from the perspective of mature grief you appreciate God's faithfulness to you throughout the physical, emotional, and spiritual trials of loss and pain. Entrusting is an investment of your personal capital. Like all investments, there is some risk. Yet there is no better trustee than God, your faithful Creator.

Prayer: God, you are the faithful Creator. I see you reflected in life all around me. May I risk the investment of entrusting myself wholly to your loving care. Amen.

Assurance: **I will continue to do good as I rebuild trust.**

Day 6

And for this reason I suffer as I do. But I am not ashamed, for I know the one in whom I have put my trust, and I am sure that he is able to guard until that day what I have entrusted to him.
2 Timothy 1:12 NRSV

Thought: Learning again to trust yourself is born of three things: desiring hope, longing for joy, and receiving peace. When you trust with all of your heart, you trust in expectation. When you trust in expectation, you trust with belief. The rebirth of trusting yourself is daring to accept God's love and trusting in God's goodness.

Prayer: God, you are the one in whom I put my trust. I am grateful for the assurance that you guard my soul within the trust of yours. Amen.

Assurance: **I entrust my life to the guardianship of God.**

Day 7 – Rest for Your Soul

Let me hear of your steadfast love in the morning,
for in you I put my trust. Teach me the way
I should go, for to you I lift up my soul.
Psalm 143:8 NRSV

Thought: You claim personal triumph over the emotional debilitation of grief when you learn to trust in yourself again. This is also a teachable moment of grief. Only when you open yourself to the risk of trust can you discern the way in which you should go. On this day of rest for your soul, entrust yourself to God.

Prayer: God, I lift up my soul to you in thanksgiving for your careful instruction through grief. May I rest in you today, for in you I put my trust. Amen.

Assurance: **My soul is still in the quiet of trust.**

Week 4 – Life

Day 1

*Trust in the L*ORD *forever, for in the L*ORD *G*OD
you have an everlasting rock.
Isaiah 26:4 NRSV

Thought: With the death of your loved one, you have been wounded. If you ever have suffered physical or emotional injury and pain because of another, you well know how difficult it is to rebuild trust. For a while you may feel violated, as if a part of yourself has been taken away from you and destroyed. Similarly, this is the experience of grief. Life has taken away someone dear and precious to you. How do you ever trust life again?

Prayer: God, in you I have an everlasting rock. I pray that you will help me to trust in you forever and again trust life. Amen.

Assurance: **I rejoice that everlasting is forever.**

Day 2

Moreover, it is required of stewards that they be found trustworthy.
1 Corinthians 4:2 NRSV

Thought: God has entrusted to you the greatest of all gifts: the gift of life. You are the steward of your life. You are in charge of how you use it and how you spend it. A trustworthy steward has a single-minded commitment to the highest and best use of that which has been entrusted. Grief inspires stewardship of your life because you have experienced the opposite extreme—the death of your loved one. Live in the trust of stewardship.

Prayer: God, because I have grieved in death I better appreciate the gift of life. May I live in gratitude as a trustworthy steward. Amen.

Assurance: **I will use the gift of life entrusted to my stewardship both wisely and well.**

Day 3

*I know, O L*ORD*, that the way of human beings is not in their control,*
that mortals as they walk cannot direct their steps.
Jeremiah 10:23 NRSV

Thought: Grief is an experience that disables your sense of control in life. Perhaps one of the most sobering realities of death is that you are not in control. You are not in charge of anyone or anything except your own attitudes and emotions. No matter how much you loved the one whose loss you grieve, you could not control either life or death. God is God. God is in control. God is life. Trust in God. Trust in life.

Prayer: God, I have learned through the experience of grief that I am not in control of anything except my own spirit. Thank you for the lesson of trust. I must trust you for direction in my life. Amen.

Assurance: **I trust in life because God is in control.**

Day 4

Teach me knowledge and good judgment,
for I trust your commands.
Psalm 119:66 NIV

Thought: An intrinsic part of trust is obedience. You expect a child or a dog to be obedient, but spiritual obedience is a seldom-praised discipline reinforced by grief. After all, grief is not only a journey of the heart; it is a life-learning experience in trust. You learn, in the words of the old familiar hymn, to "trust and obey." Or perhaps you learn knowledge and good judgment, and then you obey and trust.

Prayer: God, I trust your commands. In grief I have felt your call to obedience and trust. I am grateful for your trust of knowledge and good judgment. Amen.

Assurance: **When God commands, I obey in trust.**

Day 5

Those who trust in the LORD *are like Mount Zion,*
which cannot be moved, but abides for ever.
Psalm 125:1 ESV

Thought: Mount Zion is a geographic elevation, but the psalmist uses it here as a powerful image of unshakeable trust. It is almost impossible to move a mountain, a permanent part of the landscape formed by eons of natural creation. A mountain will not be moved by human force or will. Trust that is like Mount Zion cannot be moved by anyone or anything, not even grief. It simply is.

Prayer: God, may my trust in you grow and abide forever. I am grateful for the assurance that trust cannot be moved. Amen.

Assurance: **The majesty of nature is a visual affirmation of my trust in God.**

Day 6

I wait for the LORD, my soul waits,
and in his word I hope.
Psalm 130:5 NRSV

Thought: Even under the best of circumstances, waiting for life to happen is a test of patience. There is perhaps no spiritual discipline more difficult than patience. Patience is a gift of grief taught by grief. It is listening—"Be still, and know that I am God!" (Psalm 46:10 NRSV) Patience is waiting in trust upon God's will for your life. Patience requires trust. Patience demands that you trust life. In trust there is patience to wait on God.

Prayer: God, through your grace at last I feel ready to move away from grief. Yet for now, going forward seems to be about waiting. I pray for patience as my soul waits for you. Amen.

Assurance: **My hope is embedded within patience and trust.**

Day 7 – Rest for Your Soul

Cast your burden on the LORD,
and he will sustain you;
he will never permit
the righteous to be moved.
Psalm 55:22 NRSV

Thought: If you fish or know someone who does, perhaps you have seen the moment of release when a line is cast upward and outward. It hovers for a moment over the surface of the water until gravity inevitably forces its descent into the unknown depths. Similarly, when you cast your burden on the Lord, this is the casting motion of grief. You release your pain and the remnants of grief in a moment of exquisite trust in God and in life. Grief is cast Godward in certain trust that God is at the end of the line.

Prayer: God, on this day of rest for my soul I cast the burden of my grief on you. I trust in you, the giver of life. Amen.

Assurance: **My sustained trust in God will strengthen me for life.**

Perspective

Your kingdom is an everlasting kingdom,
and your dominion endures through all generations.
The LORD is trustworthy in all he promises
and faithful in all he does.
Psalm 145:13 NIV

Thought: In grief, trust is fragile. For a while you retreat from trust to question its place in your life. You assess the value of trust. Do you trust that God has a plan for your life beyond the pain of grief? Can you release your mistrust of others and embrace flawed relationships? Can you trust yourself as a competent person only temporarily disabled by the experience of grief? Can you open your heart and spirit to trust life again? Grief is a tenacious thief of trust. Move toward life; trust in God.

Prayer: God, you have been trustworthy to all generations and will continue to be so for as long as your everlasting kingdom endures. I am grateful for your faithfulness to me as I trust anew in life and in you. Amen.

Assurance: **God's promises are trustworthy.**

Grief Is Trust

_____

_____

_____

_____

_____

_____

_____

_____

_____

_____

_____

_____

_____

_____

_____

_____

_____

_____

GRIEF IS FAITH

Leighton aspired to be his best for all people at all times, and by doing so he inspired the best in the character and behavior of others. He lived each day actively following the example of Jesus Christ in witness to God's love, mercy, and grace at work in the world. He was a good and godly man. He trusted in God with all of his heart. He lived his faith.

When he got sick, as we prayed together each day, I assumed the role of leader. I was an amateur in the shadow of this spiritual titan now so needy and dependent on my spiritual resources and stamina. I realized over time that I could not appropriate his faith or claim it as my own. It was time to step up and prove the substance of my faith instead of relying on his.

From the onset of his illness, Leighton spent hours in bed at home, thinking, meditating, and contemplating his life and possible death. Seldom did Leighton entreat others to pray for him. When he did, the prayer that he requested was for calmness of spirit. He lived his faith with a remarkable, biblical absence of worry. He had every matter of the soul and spirit completely resolved in his private, very personal relationship with God. He was a man at peace.

For me, it was an outward paradox that a man of such immense spiritual depth and lifelong service to God, a man who had ministered with care and comfort to countless families for over fifty years and had prayed at the bedside of the sick and dying, could not will his enormous faith to shine through the darkness of his own illness and, somehow, visibly prevail at the end. Did I expect to see his inner light or hear some brilliant benediction? Perhaps I needed this mortal evidence—some proof of our immortality—for my own comfort. He was too sick to transcend infirmity, to live on some exalted spiritual plane and nobly triumph over illness for my benefit. He had the grace to bear the pain and endure it until his last breath. This is how he lived. This is how he died. He was not afraid of death. He steadfastly lived his faith until the end of his mortal life and at the last he most surely triumphed over death.

Leighton rarely marked or made notes in his Bibles. Among the books I took home from his office a few days after he died was his copy of The New Testament in Modern English, by J.B. Phillips. He admired this version for its scholarly translation, and he used it often. With his indispensable red bookkeeping pencil, he had put parentheses around the following verses, which summarize his faith and who he was:

Yes, and I shall go on being very happy, for I know that what is happening will be for the good of my own soul, thanks to your prayers and the resources of the Spirit of Jesus Christ. It all accords with my own earnest wishes and hopes, which are that I should never be in any way ashamed, that now, as always, I should honor Christ with the utmost boldness by the way I live, whether that means I am to face death or go on living. For living to me means simply 'Christ,' and if I die I should merely gain more of him. (Philippians 1:18-21 JBP)

Preparation

Now faith is the assurance of things hoped for, the conviction of things not seen.
Hebrews 11:1 NRSV

Thought: Grief is faith. Faith is the elevator of trust. Faith is the light of God that guides your way through the dark passage of grief. Faith helps you see that death is a part of life and not a catastrophe aimed at you alone. In grief, faith teaches that you must learn to die if you would learn to live. When your belief about death is grounded in faith, then and only then can you live in soul-saturating peace and joy.

Prayer: God, I know that faith includes trust and yet is so much more than trust alone. Although I cannot see it, I am certain of your love. Grow my faith as I mature away from grief. Amen.

Assurance: **God is transforming my grief into a deeper, richer faith.**

Week 1 – Prayer

Day 1

Then when you call upon me and come and pray to me, I will hear you.
Jeremiah 29:12 NRSV

Thought: Perhaps you have realized that one of the most confusing spiritual aspects of grief is prayer. When your emotions are in turmoil, usually your mind is in chaos. Likely your thoughts are a jumble of anything and everything imaginable. You want to pray, yet you cannot find that peaceful place from within to offer your broken heart to God. Because you are consumed by grief, it is difficult to focus the mind and spirit to pray. The random prayers of grief make perfect sense to God.

Prayer: God, I come to you with a heart in need of prayer. When I call upon you, I know that you hear, even when my prayers are fleeting and confused. Amen.

Assurance: **Within my silence there is prayer; within my prayer there is faith.**

Day 2

Then I called on the name of the LORD: "O LORD, I pray, save my life!"
Psalm 116:4 NRSV

Thought: In grief, you may resist the innate need to pray, yet your every thought may be a form of prayer. For a while you may be unable to ask or receive in prayer. Your prayer receptors seem broken. One way you may pray through grief is in unbroken "stream of consciousness" conversation with God, rather than a formal ritual at a predetermined time of day. Even before you ask, you listen for the answer to your plea, "O Lord, save my life!" God hears every prayer of your heart.

Prayer: God, you have saved my life through all the days of my grief. I am grateful that my soul calls on your name continuously, even when my spirit is distracted by grief. Amen.

Assurance: **I know that my prayers are answered.**

Day 3

Now, O my God, let your eyes be open and your ears
attentive to prayer from this place.
2 Chronicles 6:40 NRSV

Thought: Because of the experience of death, your expectations of prayer may change. When you watch a loved one die, you may be spiritually immobilized by your own helplessness. In the urgent quiet of desperation, you may be unable to pray. Your fervent, whispered pleas for healing and restoration are answered, but not with yes. You learn that the answer to prayer may be wait or no. When you pray for comfort and strength, however, the answer is always yes.

Prayer: God, even when I am not attentive to you, I know that you listen and hear my prayers. Thank you for the assurance that you are with me at this place now. Amen.

Assurance: **Wherever I pray, whatever I pray, I believe that God hears and answers me.**

Day 4

Answer me when I call, O God of my right!
You gave me room when I was in distress.
Be gracious to me, and hear my prayer.
Psalm 4:1 NRSV

Thought: Why do you pray? You pray because God asks you to share your inmost being through prayer. You pray because God cares for you, because God is interested in every detail of your life. You pray not to enlighten God but to discern the mind of God. Prayer draws you closer to God; it deepens your relationship with God. It is a humbling moment of grief when prayer reminds you that you are dependent on God and not on yourself.

Prayer: God, you are gracious to me. I am grateful that you have given me spiritual room to grieve even as I open my heart to you in prayer. Amen.

Assurance: **Prayer alleviates my spiritual weariness.**

Day 5

The LORD has heard my supplication;
the LORD accepts my prayer.
Psalm 6:9 NRSV

Thought: Friends and family assure you that they are praying for you. If you feel unable to pray, you may allow the prayers of others to carry you for as long as you feel disconnected from God. It is not so much that you are unwilling to pray; when you grieve, often you are unable to offer more than the simplest expression of prayer. Through prayer, as in grief, you grow spiritually; you are transformed and renewed. When you, in turn, pray for others, you abandon self-involvement and acknowledge spiritual needs beyond the horizon of your own grief.

Prayer: God, I know that you hear my prayers. Thank you for accepting my prayers, however disjointed and simple they may be. Amen.

Assurance: **When I pray, I surrender my will to God's will.**

Day 6

Therefore let all who are faithful
offer prayer to you;
at a time of distress, the rush of mighty waters
shall not reach them.
Psalm 32:6 NRSV

Thought: In grief, persistent questions invade every area of your emotional and spiritual well-being. To better understand prayer, consider your personal retrospective. What did you pray for if you watched illness progressing toward death? What was the answer to your prayer? Do you believe that your prayers for healing were not answered? At the death of your loved one, how did you respond to the answer to your prayer—anger, disappointment, resentment, bewilderment? As a defining part of faith, prayer is always available, whatever the answer may be.

Prayer: God, even through the distress of grief, the force of grief has not overwhelmed me. May I release my questions to you in faithful prayer. Amen.

Assurance: **Prayer repels the rush of grief's mighty waters.**

Day 7 – Rest for Your Soul

"Whatever you ask for in prayer with faith, you will receive."
Matthew 21:22 NRSV

Thought: God knows what you need before you pray. God asks only that you lift your broken heart in prayer that is soul-searching and introspective; in prayer that allows listening and meditation; in prayer that is possible only within the silence of the heart; in prayer for divine wisdom and insight.

Prayer: God, on this day of rest my heart and mind are attuned to you. I ask in faith for your soul-sustaining grace, knowing that it is mine to receive. Amen.

Assurance: **God listens; I know that God is always there for me.**

Week 2 – Courage

Day 1

For we walk by faith, not by sight.
2 Corinthians 5:7 RSV

Thought: Courage is heroic and inspiring. The word *courage* is derived from the Latin word cor, meaning "heart." Courage is your outward response to your inner fear; it is your fear turned inside out. In grief, you transform fear into courage by doing that which you fear. Then you become stronger. Your simultaneous challenge is to deconstruct fear and reconstruct courage in faith. What are your fears that need to be expressed as courage?

Prayer: God, grief is, indeed, a test of courage. I pray for faith to walk fearlessly with you into the unknown way ahead. Amen.

Assurance: **The faithfulness of God fortifies my courage.**

Day 2

Keep alert, stand firm in your faith, be courageous, be strong.
1 Corinthians 16:13 NRSV

Thought: The spirit that enables you to face difficulty without fear is bravery. Bravery is the bold, intrepid courage inspired by the love of God—your citadel and the bastion of your faith. In grief, bravery may be weak and tentative. Yet when you dare those conscious acts that test your courage, your faith is rewarded in dividends of confidence and hope.

Prayer: God, it is difficult to be brave when I am weak and fearful. Inspire my heart with the courage of your love. Amen.

Assurance: **I will be courageous and stand firm in my faith.**

Day 3

Only be strong and very courageous.
Joshua 1:7 NRSV

Thought: Acts of brute courage require bravery to defeat the persistent fears of grief. When you succeed at bravery, you feel as though you deserve a medal or some outward acknowledgment of your courage. You find that your strength is renewed as you courageously venture from your place of pervasive woundedness to gradually rejoin the world.

Prayer: God, to be very courageous I need your unfailing strength. May I live with the courage of faith enlarged by grief. Amen.

Assurance: **Courage and strength are the inseparable allies of my faith.**

Day 4

Each one helps the other, saying to one another, "Take courage!"
Isaiah 41:6 NRSV

Thought: As you recapture the bravery to live forward in faith, you begin to seek the best part of courage: encouragement. When you share your grief with others who have experienced the death of a loved one, you recognize that you are not alone. You are encouraged by the support of community in your grief. Who or what gives you encouragement? From whom or what do you receive spiritual encouragement?

Prayer: God, there is power in the encouragement of others. I am grateful for the connection of faith in you. Amen.

Assurance: **Fortitude and faith inspire my newfound courage.**

Day 5

"Keep up your courage!"
Acts 23:11 NRSV

Thought: It is one thing to have a moment of bravery or an isolated experience of courage, but it is quite another to actually keep up your courage—that is, to live in the sustained courage that becomes not only a habit but also a way of life. Grief is among the most discouraging passages of life. Reclaimed courage is a triumph of faith.

Prayer: God, I long to live in sustained courage so that every day is a victory over grief. Thank you for the encouragement of exclamation. Amen.

Assurance: **When I keep up my courage, I live in faith.**

Day 6

"But you, take courage! Do not let your hands be weak,
for your work shall be rewarded."
2 Chronicles 15:7 NRSV

Thought: It gets your attention when someone points a finger and says "you." The encouragement of the Bible is as real today as it was centuries ago. It is personal. It is meant for you. Grief is the work of bravery, courage, and restoration. Grief takes an effort; it is the individual work of your two strong hands held in faith by God.

Prayer: God, you strengthen my hands and heart for the work of grief. I am grateful that your call for courage is personal, meant for me. Amen.

Assurance: **My renewed courage is a reward of my grief.**

Day 7 – Rest for Your Soul

For whatever was written in former days was written for our instruction, so
that by steadfastness and by the encouragement of the
scriptures we might have hope.
Romans 15:4 NRSV

Thought: In courage your spirit is reborn as slowly you find your way back into life. You live again, resurrected from grief through acts of courage that transform your grief into a greater living faith. When you receive the promise of hope, you are blessed with steadfast strength through the encouragement of the scriptures.

Prayer: God, on this day of rest my soul is rekindled with courage. Thank you for your steadfast instruction of my heart in grief. Amen.

Assurance: **My courage is from the hope of faith.**

Week 3 – Reconstruction

Day 1

Unless the LORD builds the house,
those who build it labor in vain.
Psalm 127:1 NRSV

Thought: A contractor or building design specialist likely would agree that it is easier to build a new structure than remodel an old one. Buildings usually decline into functional obsolescence after a period of use if not updated or modernized to current standards. Construction teems with positive energy. The smell of fresh sawdust suggests the promise of a completed project, sparkling and new at the end. Reconstruction acknowledges the existence of something worth salvaging. It carefully honors the remaining life within a structure, regardless of its condition. In grief, that structure is your very life.

Prayer: God, I have struggled through grief to rebuild my life. Yet often my labor is in vain when I quest after that which is not of your creation. I pray that you will rebuild my life according to your plan. Amen.

Assurance: **I will begin the reconstruction of my life today.**

Day 2

"For which of you, intending to build a tower, does not first sit down and esti-
mate the cost, to see whether he has enough to complete it? Otherwise, when
he has laid a foundation and is not able to finish, all who see it will begin to
ridicule him, saying, 'This fellow began to build and was not able to finish.'"
Luke 14:28-30 NRSV

Thought: Throughout the journey of grief, likely you have considered from time to time what it would take to rebuild your life. Are you willing to expend the effort for an unknown future? Do you have the stamina, discipline, and will to complete personal reconstruction? Are you influenced by the judgment and opinion of others in rebuilding a new life of your own design? Do you have the determination to work at your own pace toward some unknown completion date, perhaps sooner or maybe later? When you have a foundation, you are ready to rebuild.

Prayer: God, I prayerfully wonder whether I have what it takes to rebuild my life. I question my energy, resolve, and even the length of my life. With you as the foundation, I begin in faith. Amen.

Assurance: **I will sit down, estimate the cost, and then build my life anew.**

Day 3

*"The rain fell, the floods came, and the winds blew and beat on that house, but
it did not fall, because it had been founded on rock."*
Matthew 7:25 NRSV

Thought: The most essential part of any structure is a sound foundation. When
your life is deconstructed by death, your structure may seem near total collapse.
The tremors of loss quake the bedrock of your soul. Yet you stand, your footing
secured by the unshakeable foundation that never fails. The sacred ground on
which you rebuild cannot be destroyed. It is indestructible.

Prayer: God, you are the foundation on which I build. I am grateful that you
never fall, you never fail, and you never change. Amen.

Assurance: **The faithfulness of God is the rock on which I resolve to build.**

Day 4

*Go through, go through the gates,
prepare the way for the people;
build up, build up the highway,
clear it of stones.*
Isaiah 62:10 NRSV

Thought: When your loved one died, the ordered structure of life was razed, destroyed with a single, final breath. In a mere second, the labor of love and personal
investment of a lifetime together were reduced to a pile of twisted rubble—the
remains an odd admixture of dusty, unusable material. Rebuilding to accommodate life without your loved one requires that you prepare by clearing away the
remains of the past that do not belong to the future. As you move forward, you
discover that your personal reconstruction project stimulates both your mind and
heart. In faith you contemplate practically endless possibilities for new life.

Prayer: God, after the destruction of grief, I hear you say, "Build up, build up."
I hesitate to go through the door to new life. May I get ready, begin, and rebuild
in faith. Amen.

Assurance: **I will prepare the site for building my new life.**

Day 5

*For everything there is a season, and a time for every matter under heaven:
a time to be born, and a time to die;*
. . . .
a time to break down, and a time to build up.
Ecclesiastes 3:1-3 NRSV

Thought: Some basic principles of construction must be followed for the success of your rebuilding project. There is a plan to follow. There is a design, either conventional or free-form. There are construction steps that must occur in sequential order. As structure takes form, the plan may change. Your structure may be altered by circumstance—remarriage, infirmity, or even death. You change the plan; you try again. You build forward. You reorder your life so that it feels like a comfortable, emotional home.

Prayer: God, in grief I understand better the order and rhythm of life, even in death. I am grateful that through your grace I am at last ready for the season to build up. Amen.

Assurance: **I am rebuilding my life into a place I want to live.**

Day 6

"I will show you what someone is like who comes to me, hears my words, and acts on them. That one is like a man building a house, who dug deeply and laid the foundation on rock; when a flood arose, the river burst against that house but could not shake it, because it had been well built."
Luke 6:47-48 NRSV

Thought: The hands of a construction worker usually show the wear and tear of daily use. Seldom is a good worker without a bruise under the fingernail, the silent badge of handwork. In grief, you are similarly bruised under your emotional exterior. You perhaps put on figurative gloves to protect yourself from contact, commitment, or the inevitable march of progress through your life. As with a physical bruise, the injury of grief usually improves over time. When you are ready to begin, you roll up your sleeves and do the hands-on work of rebuilding your structure. Personal growth propels your project forward as gradually you build, carefully placing one block of experience upon the last. Your self-renewal project takes form and shape. An improved structure emerges from the building materials of grief. The work is messy and dirty, but construction is always productive.

Prayer: God, you are the master carpenter. I come to you ready to rebuild, ready to act on your words of instruction. May I dig deeply from within and lay my foundation on your rock. Amen.

Assurance: **Completing the hard work of reconstruction requires my aptitude and commitment.**

Day 7 – Rest for Your Soul

For we are God's servants, working together;
you are God's field, God's building.
1 Corinthians 3:9 NRSV

Thought: Reconstruction is the work of self-nurture. You honor your body with proper care so that your new structure is physically and emotionally sound. You eliminate self-destructive behavior. You affirm yourself for who you are. You recognize the gifts and graces that are yours to offer in service to God and others. You partner with God; you build on the rock.

Prayer: God, I am your servant. May I work with you to be your building, rebuilt from grief and dedicated to a life of gratitude. Amen.

Assurance: **Faith inspires me to do the work of grief in my personal reconstruction.**

Week 4 – Eternity

Day 1

Therefore, since we are justified by faith, we have peace with
God through our Lord Jesus Christ.
Romans 5:1 NRSV

Thought: For many Christians, grief is sometimes framed in self-denial. Those who feel guilty for crying or being sad may believe that a person of strong faith should feel happy to know that a loved one is in heaven. You can believe beyond doubt that a loved one is with God, but you are human. You are in pain. You hurt. This does not mean that you are a bad Christian or that your faith is weak. It means that grief and faith are connected in Christ. "And without faith it is impossible to please God, for whoever would approach him must believe that he exists and that he rewards those who seek him" (Hebrews 11:6 NRSV).

Prayer: God, as my faith grows because of grief, I pray for peace through your grace in Christ. Amen.

Assurance: **My faith pleases God.**

Day 2

For by grace you have been saved through faith, and this is not
your own doing; it is the gift of God.
Ephesians 2:8 NRSV

Thought: Pain and sorrow are vanquished by faith. Death is rendered powerless as you, at last, pass through the valley of the shadow of death in full faith and grief is no more. Death does not leave you ambivalent in your resolve to claim new life in the victory over death. God's saving grace through Christ is freely given to you through faith. Thanks be to God for the gift of life and eternity. "The righteousness of God is revealed through faith for faith; as it is written, 'The one who is righteous will live by faith' " (Romans 1:17 NRSV).

Prayer: God, I have done nothing to merit or earn your saving grace. May I receive it with a heart of faith in gratitude for Christ. Amen.

Assurance: **I will live by faith.**

Day 3

Examine yourselves to see whether you are living in the faith. Test yourselves. Do you not realize that Jesus Christ is in you?
2 Corinthians 13:5 NRSV

Thought: As you continue moving toward the end of grief, you may want to consider a personal inventory of who you are becoming along the way of your journey. Who are you in your inmost heart? What are the qualities of your soul? How would you describe yourself? How would you characterize who you are? Do you think that others see the same qualities in you? Do you believe one way yet live another? Are you living in greater faith because of grief? "Faith comes from what is heard, and what is heard comes through the word of Christ" (Romans 10:17 NRSV).

Prayer: God, holding up the mirror of faith to my grief-worn heart is a test of Christ in me. I pray that I am living in faith more and more with each new day. Amen.

Assurance: **I live in faith because Christ is in me.**

Day 4

But someone will say, "You have faith and I have works." Show me your faith apart from your works, and I by my works will show you my faith.
James 2:18 NRSV

Thought: Faith and works are partners in Christ. Faith without works is mere rhetoric. It does little good only to talk about faith. "So faith by itself, if it has no works, is dead" (James 2:17 NRSV). The power of faith comes from living in faithfulness to God. It is demonstrating your faith to others in good works. As a response to grace, faith is an active, breathing force. It is the pulse of your spiritual life.

Prayer: God, it requires little to speak of faith; it demands far more to live by faith. May my works in your name reflect the faith of my heart. Amen.

Assurance: **I live my faith through works.**

Day 5

Fight the good fight of the faith; take hold of the eternal life,
to which you were called.
1 Timothy 6:12 NRSV

Thought: In grief, you come to understand that if God has arranged for birth and life, God has arranged equally well for death and grief. Death is not termination but transition. Death is not the end of life. Rather, death is an eternal transaction. As you say farewell here on earth, God says welcome on the distant shore. When there is night here, somewhere else there is dawn. The God of your faith is the God of eternity. Eternal life is worth the good fight of faith. "I have fought the good fight, I have finished the race, I have kept the faith" (2 Timothy 4:7 NRSV).

Prayer: God, I am called by your grace to eternal life in Christ. Thank you for the strength to fight the good fight of faith. Amen.

Assurance: **I am fighting the good fight of faith.**

Day 6

We look not at what can be seen but at what cannot be seen; for what can be
seen is temporary, but what cannot be seen is eternal.
2 Corinthians 4:18 NRSV

Thought: Though you cannot prove it, likely you have had evidence of the abiding spiritual presence of your loved one in some way that affirms the reality of the unseen. Perhaps something occurred that you know without question was an un-mistakable sign or signal that you alone would understand. Its power and force affirmed to you the real, eternal presence of your loved one. For now, the reality of the unseen is a mystery. It is God's mystery of life and death. God's unseen reality is eternal life, which is the very promise of faith. "By faith we understand that the worlds were prepared by the word of God, so that what is seen was made from things that are not visible" (Hebrews 11:3 NRSV).

Prayer: God, may I look in faith to that which cannot be seen, to all that is eternal in you. I am grateful for the reality of the unseen that strengthens my faith and heart. Amen.

Assurance: **By faith I believe in the unseen reality of eternal life.**

Day 7 – Rest for Your Soul

"Very truly, I tell you, anyone who hears my word and believes him who sent me has eternal life, and does not come under judgment, but has passed from death to life."
John 5:24 NRSV

Thought: Faith is belief without evidence. The modern world constantly bombards you with ideas and suggestions that you hear and accept, likely at face value. But do you believe everything you hear? The message of God's saving grace in Christ is the faith of belief without evidence. In eternal life there is life without death. "And this is the testimony: God gave us eternal life, and this life is in his Son" (1 John 5:11 NRSV).

Prayer: God, on this day of rest for my soul, I rejoice in the gift of eternal life. I am grateful that in you, death passes to life. Amen.

Assurance: **I am grateful for the gift of eternal life in Christ.**

Perspective

Whatever is born of God conquers the world. And this is the victory that conquers the world, our faith.
1 John 5:4 NRSV

Thought: As you mature in faith through grief, you learn more about the need for prayer and the effect of prayer in the quiet of your soul. You rediscover courage through the power of encouragement. You are encouraged, and in faith you extend your heart to encourage others. You begin to rebuild your life again. Reconstruction is the work of faith. In the saving grace of God through Christ, you receive the victory that conquers the world. This is the life of faith beyond the broken heart. "And we know that the Son of God has come and has given us understanding so that we may know him who is true; and we are in him who is true, in his Son Jesus Christ. He is the true God and eternal life" (1 John 5:20 NRSV).

Prayer: God, on the journey through grief you have kept the faith with me. May I serve you in the world with the mature faith cultivated by grief. Amen.

Assurance: **In my faith there is victory over death and grief.**

Grief Is Faith

GRIEF IS LOVE

In the early days of our romance, people asked me about Leighton. They wanted to know what he was like. The first thing that came to mind was that he was a person of authentic goodness. He was genuine. He was pure in heart. He was always and absolutely the same person. He was no different in public than he was in private.

Leighton had an infectious sense of humor and a staccato laugh that rose in crescendo from somewhere deep within his body. Jokes told from the pulpit and those reserved for more private moments delighted those who were privileged to experience this unexpected dimension of his rather serious personality. Those who knew him thought he was fun and funny. The grandsons called him Funny Boy. Leighton and I loved to laugh, to put our heads together in mirthful, intimate abandon—not laughing at, just laughing.

I let go of a part of my fierce self-determination and independence to be blessed by our marriage. Ours was not a love of sublimation or subjugation. Ours was a love for all time. Leighton was not a master; rather, he was masterful at being my husband. Having lived most of my adult life alone, I was independent. He understood that the best way to hold onto me, to keep me close, was to bless my individuality so that I might become who I was yet to be.

We loved as one, unconditionally, with nothing held back. Ours was a love that made life bubble, sparkle, and shine. We were true soul mates—the masculine and feminine sides of the same coin made of the purest, most refined gold: that of true love. This is the love that makes grief so profound. We loved at the risk of losing it all. We loved large. I lost large, yet I would never change the risk-to-loss ratio of love, even for the pain of grief.

When he got sick, Leighton could not be present to me emotionally with the same passion and devotion of love he so faithfully lavished on me over the years of our marriage. Throughout his illness he relied on me, presuming that my love would be sufficient for us both. After he died, I felt a plea from beyond to forgive him the enormous pain I suffered as he withdrew into himself before death, which so added to my grief. He never could have known, nor could he have imagined, the power of grief unless it had been I who had become sick and died.

It took years for me to work through the "why" of it all, which for me was more about reflection than forgiveness. We should have done so much so differently. Leighton surely forgave me my insufficiencies to his illness and death. I could not fix it. I could not save him. At last my self-reproach was silenced by a small whisper within, "Peace! Be still!" (Mark 4:39 NRSV) There was spiritual calm in that moment of forgiveness—of myself, of him, and of others. It's all forgiven, long ago. It's in the past. In forgiveness there is freedom.

In grief I have warred within myself over the hierarchies of love in my life. Leighton and I loved each other with the complete devotion that is a stronghold in my heart forever. I have asked myself whether my love for Leighton supplanted my love for God. Did I idolize the man rather than worship God? No, love is. One love does not exclude the other. It is not "either/or." They coexist. Through my journey of grief, I have come to understand better that the nature of God's love is not ownership, even as we love God first with all our heart, mind, soul, and strength. God's love does not control or limit us; rather, it frees and encourages us to grow in love, both mortal and divine.

Now I obsess less, remember always, and love forever. Leighton is alive in my heart. Our love will never die. His dying and death in no way affect my love. It never has; it never could. For love outlasts everything.

Preparation

Beloved, let us love one another, because love is from God.
1 John 4:7a NRSV

Thought: At the heart of grief is love. Love is from God and therefore eternal. We love because God first loved us. God's love is for us all and is over all. God's love is all-inclusive, abundant, and infinite. If you love, you live in the nature of

God. As with love, death is a part of life. Death has not parted you from your loved one. In love you are bound together forever, because love never dies.

Prayer: God, grief illuminates your presence as the source of all love. I am grateful for love, your indwelling spirit. Amen.

Assurance: **Love is from God.**

Week 1 – Durable Love

Day 1

Love knows no limit to its endurance, no end to its trust, no fading of its hope;
it can outlast anything. It is, in fact, the one thing that still
stands when all else has fallen.
1 Corinthians 13:7-8 JBP

Thought: Love is the one thing that still stands when all else has fallen. You find the spiritual basis of durable love in the biblical assurance that God is love. If you know that God is love and that God ordains love, then you believe that love can outlast anything. The love you shared with your loved one transcends the event of death. This is the absolute power of love.

Prayer: God, your love has held me up through grief and keeps me from falling. I am grateful that your love is infinite and forever. Amen.

Assurance: **Love has no limits.**

Day 2

For the LORD is good;
his steadfast love endures for ever,
and his faithfulness to all generations.
Psalm 100:5 NRSV

Thought: In the sanctity of relationship, you create a legacy of love that becomes part of who you are. It begs to be given away with abandon to those you love and those in need of hope and encouragement. Your love lives on—and on and on—when you invest in others. This is your unique, personal legacy of love to future generations.

Prayer: God, everlasting love is the heritage of faith. I am grateful for the rich inheritance of your love for all generations. Amen.

Assurance: **Steadfast love is faithful.**

Day 3

With everlasting love I will have compassion on you,
says the LORD, your Redeemer.
Isaiah 54:8 NRSV

Thought: Compassion is born of love. Grief urges you to greater compassion for the heartache of others. You model compassion in your spiritual reaction to life's trials and tragedies, especially grief. Indeed, a heightened sense of compassion is a gift of grief. When you reach out in love with a heart fortified from within by your experience of grief, you show what God is like. You are a benefactor of compassion.

Prayer: God, throughout grief you have shown me your everlasting love and compassion. As I move beyond my broken heart, may I serve you with compassion for others. Amen.

Assurance: **Love sustains hope.**

Day 4

The LORD is good to all,
and his compassion is over all that he has made.
Psalm 145:9 NRSV

Thought: When you learn the hard-won lessons of humanity and compassion from grief, you are better able to join hands with others and communicate heart to heart: "I hurt with you; I share your pain; I love you." Yours is the heart and voice of emotional and spiritual authenticity. The gift of compassion offered to others is never forgotten. There is perhaps no finer legacy than to endow those you love with a sensibility for compassion.

Prayer: God, grief has shown me that compassion is at the heart of your love. I am grateful that you have touched me and taught me deep within. Amen.

Assurance: **Love stands when all else falls.**

Day 5

By day the LORD commands his steadfast love,
and at night his song is with me,
a prayer to the God of my life.
Psalm 42:8 NRSV

Thought: Though the music of life stops for a while with the death of your loved one, the song of eternal love plays forever in your heart. The melody never changes; the tune remains the same. Perhaps the patina of time adds depth to the arrangement as the setting of life changes. The echo of your shared song reverberates forever, sharing its beauty with others throughout eternity.

Prayer: God, your song of love is with me day and night. You are the God of my life. Amen.

Assurance: **The song of my life plays on.**

Day 6

How precious is your steadfast love, O God!
Psalm 36:7 NRSV

Thought: Though death robs you of the presence and companionship of your loved one, it never can steal the precious love you shared together. That place of inner sanctum always will be part of who you are, whatever the future. Your life journey is greater, richer, and fuller for having loved the one lost to you in death. The time and space you share in love is both sacred and eternal.

Prayer: God, your steadfast love assures me that love cannot be taken away or destroyed, even by death. I am grateful for the precious gift of love. Amen.

Assurance: **I am created to love and to be loved.**

Day 7 – Rest for Your Soul

For your steadfast love is before my eyes,
and I walk in faithfulness to you.
Psalm 26:3 NRSV

Thought: Though with death you lose sight of your loved one, love is always in plain view. Death only separates; it does not take love away. In grief slowly you realize that nothing is lost or compromised if you release your tenacious emotional grip and relax into the certainty that love is. Love never fails.

Prayer: God, on this day of rest my soul walks in the faithfulness of your love. I am grateful that your love is ever before me. Amen.

Assurance: **Love can outlast anything.**

Week 2 – God's Love

Day 1

Everyone who loves is born of God and knows God.
1 John 4:7b NRSV

Thought: God uses grief to teach you more about God's love. Consider how you see God's love reflected through you. Although you are not responsible for how or whether your love is received, you alone determine the way in which you express and give it. When you love without expectation, you leave the results to God.

Prayer: God, you endow me with life and love. May I know you more in the grace of love. Amen.

Assurance: **I am a reflection of God's great love.**

Day 2

Whoever does not love does not know God, for God is love.
1 John 4:8 NRSV

Thought: A world without love is unimaginable. Grief either affirms your certainty of God's abiding love or leaves you embittered and broken, depending on how you react to the intrinsic spiritual power of this life-changing experience. It is impossible to be apathetic about love. Its opposite emotions are dark but equally strong. There is life-renewing strength in the power of love—God's love for you.

Prayer: God, you show me the power of love for life beyond grief. I am grateful that your love exceeds all human thought and imagination. Amen.

Assurance: **Because I love, I know God.**

Day 3

God's love was revealed among us in this way: God sent his only Son into the world so that we might live through him.
1 John 4:9 NRSV

Thought: If you could give but one gift, the greatest would be love. God sent Christ into the world so that we might fully know God's love by seeing it in action. God's gift of love was and is without reservation. God did not hold back, calculating the risk of rejection before giving this gift of love. Christ is proof of God's love for you.

Prayer: God, I pray that I may fully receive the gift of your love and live in response to your grace in Christ. Amen.

Assurance: **God's love is revealed to me through Christ.**

Day 4

In this is love, not that we loved God but that he loved us.
1 John 4:10 NRSV

Thought: As the Creator, God loved you first. You love God in response to the love that God already has given. You cannot trump God's love through works or good deeds. You cannot out-give God even when you give your best. Though it is sometimes a temptation of grief to ignore or reject God, God's love is unconditional and resolute. Receive God's outpouring of love.

Prayer: God, your love is so incomprehensible. I give you thanks that you loved me first and that all I must do is receive. Amen.

Assurance: **God's love precedes all life.**

Day 5

Beloved, since God loved us so much, we also ought to love one another.
1 John 4:11 NRSV

Thought: God's love for you is immeasurable. Because God loves you so much, it is your privilege in gratitude to show God's love to others. Do you love with prejudice or despite your prejudice? Do you love with judgment or openly, without judgment, and solely for the sake of love? How do you react when your love is not received in the spirit in which it is given? How much do you love?

Prayer: God, it is difficult to fathom how much you love me. May the love of my heart, amplified by grief, be the love of Christ I show to others. Amen.

Assurance: **Love one another.**

Day 6

*No one has ever seen God; if we love one another, God lives
in us, and his love is perfected in us.*
1 John 4:12 NRSV

Thought: The living presence of God within you is the force of your spirit when you love others. It is the reservoir of all love. The perfection of love is predicated on loving others as much or even more than yourself. "Love your neighbor as yourself" (Leviticus 19:18 NIV). The biblical admonition is to "go on toward perfection" (Hebrews 6:1 NRSV). When God lives in you, God lives through you. You see God's love at work when you live in God's Spirit.

Prayer: God, you instruct me to love others so that your love in me may be perfected. I pray that your Spirit living in me speaks your love to others. Amen.

Assurance: **God's love is perfected in me when I love others as I love myself.**

Day 7 – Rest for Your Soul

*So we have known and believe the love that God has for us. God is love, and
those who abide in love abide in God, and God abides in them.*
1 John 4:16 NRSV

Thought: When you contemplate with introspection and gratitude your journey through grief, you recognize that where you are now is sacred evidence of God's abiding love for you. Your life in God's love before the death of your loved one is enhanced and augmented by the intense spiritual experience of God's love through grief. You know God's love from the front row of pain and sorrow. "Love the LORD your God with all your heart, and with all your soul, and with all your might. Keep these words that I am commanding you today in your heart" (Deuteronomy 6:5-6 NRSV).

Prayer: God, I believe with all of my heart in your love for me. On this day of rest may I abide with faith in your love, even as you abide in me. Amen.

Assurance: **I abide in God's love.**

Week 3 – Forgiving Yourself

Day 1

"But the one to whom little is forgiven, loves little."
Luke 7:47 NRSV

Thought: You strangle the growth of love when you cannot forgive yourself. If you hold yourself blameless throughout life, likely you look to others for the cause of most of what impacts your life negatively. The effect is small love. To grow forward in love and one day graduate from grief, you commend your experience of death to the perspective of the past, enlarged to include your humanness.

Prayer: God, it is easier to blame others for the reversals in my life. I pray that you will instruct my heart in forgiveness, so that I may forgive myself and then others. Amen.

Assurance: **I will look within to forgive myself.**

Day 2

"Occasions for stumbling are bound to come.... If there is repentance, you must forgive."
Luke 17:1, 3 NRSV

Thought: In grief it is easy to stumble over all the wrong things. Perhaps you struggle to forgive yourself for your human impotence to save your loved one from death. Or perhaps you wish that you might have offered or received a parting word of forgiveness. When you forgive yourself those things that never can be relived or changed, you free that emotional energy to invest in new life.

Prayer: God, I tenaciously hang on to that which cannot be altered. I know that you already have forgiven me my perceived and real failures. May I accept your love and forgive myself. Amen.

Assurance: **In forgiveness there is release.**

Day 3

Just as the Lord has forgiven you, so you also must forgive.
Colossians 3:13 NRSV

Thought: In grief the hardest person to forgive is yourself. You hold on to self-condemnation for a while; you are emotionally and spiritually unaccustomed to healthy self-love and self-esteem in the aftermath of the death of your loved one. Forgiveness is not optional. You must forgive yourself in order to complete the journey through grief.

Prayer: God, I am grateful for the assurance of your forgiveness. May I find in your example the inspiration to forgive myself. Amen.

Assurance: **When I forgive myself, I quiet trouble in my heart.**

Day 4

Then Peter remembered what Jesus had said: "Before the cock crows, you will deny me three times." And he went out and wept bitterly.
Matthew 26:75 NRSV

Thought: Peter claimed to be the most loyal of all the disciples. He protested loudly and energetically that he would never betray Jesus. Yet Peter was human. When he found himself alone by the fire—the only male friend who accompanied Christ to his humiliation and trial—he was quick and vehement in his denial when others confronted him about his relationship with Jesus. Jesus had foretold Peter's betrayal. When Peter heard the cock crow, he realized what he had done. Peter grieved the error of his ways constructively. He left and wept bitterly. Ultimately, he forgave himself. In the power of forgiveness, Peter lived to become the rock upon which the Christian church was built.

Prayer: God, like Peter, I am passionate in my loyalties, yet I err in my human weakness. I am grateful that tears reflect a repentant heart. Amen.

Assurance: **I will forgive myself and live forward in forgiveness.**

Day 5

When Judas, his betrayer, saw that Jesus was condemned, he repented and brought back the thirty pieces of silver to the chief priests and the elders.
Matthew 27:3 NRSV

Thought: Judas committed the ultimate betrayal. His infamy is the historic standard for treachery. After the deed, which was committed for money, Judas did not have the spiritual wherewithal to forgive himself. He was unable to suffer productively and redeem his egregious betrayal of Christ through forgiveness.

Tragically, he succumbed to remorse through self-inflicted death rather than live with his misdeed in the humility of self-forgiveness and divine forgiveness.

Prayer: God, thank you for the precious gift of life. May I first seek forgiveness from you and then learn to forgive myself. Amen.

Assurance: **Regret is the first step in forgiveness.**

Day 6

" 'Father, I have sinned against heaven and before you;
I am no longer worthy to be called your son.' "
Luke 15:21 NRSV

Thought: In the familiar story of the prodigal son, the wayward younger son of a rich man asks for the distribution of his inheritance, leaves his father's house, and proceeds to waste his legacy on immature, immediate pleasures. When his re-sources are spent, he is reduced to a demeaning lifestyle. He realizes that he has made a big mistake, and he makes a plan to return home, hoping that his father will forgive him. Before asking his father for forgiveness, the son likely realizes he first must forgive himself. Only then is he able to take the risk that his father will welcome him back in the grace of full forgiveness.

Prayer: God, there are times when I cannot imagine that you forgive me for what I have done. I pray that you will strengthen me in the assurance that you forgive long before I forgive myself. Amen.

Assurance: **There is nothing that God will not forgive.**

Day 7 – Rest for Your Soul

The one whose wrongdoing is forgiven,
whose sin is covered over,
is truly happy!
Psalm 32:1 CEB

Thought: What does it mean to say that wrongdoing is "covered over"? It means that it is forgiven and forgotten. Forgetting your own wrongdoings, however far in the past they may be, is perhaps even more difficult than forgiving yourself. The only one remembering is you. When God forgives you and you, in turn, for-give yourself, your wrongdoings are consigned to oblivion forever. You are blessed when you forgive yourself.

Prayer: God, forgiving and forgetting my own wrongdoings is an ongoing challenge of life. On this day of rest may I allow the balm of forgiveness to saturate and bless my soul in your grace. Amen.

Assurance: **I master my grief when I forgive and forget.**

Week 4 – Forgiving Others

Day 1

"Do not judge, and you will not be judged; do not condemn, and you will not be condemned. Forgive, and you will be forgiven."
Luke 6:37 NRSV

Thought: Successfully completing the work of grief requires some basic emotional and spiritual housekeeping. With a stiff new broom you carefully, meticulously sweep every corner of your heart for unnecessary emotional debris. You dust for cobwebs of the past, collecting and clearing out stale resentments, messy ill will, judgment, and condemnation. You air out the room that is the rest of your life, restoring order and tranquility to the space of your soul. Grief is a unique opportunity to start fresh.

Prayer: God, the cause and effect of forgiveness is a dynamic of life and grief. I am grateful for the grace to forgive others, even as I am forgiven by you. Amen.

Assurance: **I will forgive others as well as myself.**

Day 2

"If you forgive the sins of any, they are forgiven them; if you retain the sins of any, they are retained."
John 20:23 NRSV

Thought: The power of forgiveness lies in its immediacy. One of the most difficult things to understand about God's forgiveness is that you ask and you receive, right then, on the spot. There is no pause for explanation or qualification, no caveats about repentance and atonement. Forgiveness is a real-time experience. It is God's grace at work in your life at that very moment.

Prayer: God, I hold back before I am ready to forgive others. I pray for the generosity of spirit to forgive others wholeheartedly and without hesitation. Amen.

Assurance: **Forgiveness is forgiving forever.**

Day 3

Be kind to one another, tenderhearted, forgiving one another,
as God in Christ has forgiven you.
Ephesians 4:32 NRSV

Thought: When you forgive others, you give the gift of grace. The embodiment of grace is the love of God in Christ. In forgiveness, your grief-hardened heart is overwhelmed by the spirit of kindness. At once it becomes tender and forgiving, eager to put the misdeeds of the past behind. There is strength and cleansing in forgiveness. This is the exit door of grief.

Prayer: God, may I be kind and tender-hearted to others, ready to forgive even as you forgive me in Christ. Amen.

Assurance: **In forgiveness I experience personal restoration.**

Day 4

"Whenever you stand praying, forgive, if you have anything against anyone; so
that your Father in heaven may also forgive you your trespasses."
Mark 11:25 NRSV

Thought: One of the heaviest loads of grief—as well as life in general—is the great ledger book of life. In forgiveness, you reconcile for a last time, then definitively shut your closely held book of accounts on the shortcomings of yourself and others. When you give up lifetime recordkeeping, you lighten the load. You offload the past and move toward the future in the light of full forgiveness.

Prayer: God, in prayer I acknowledge to you my forgiveness of others—not so that you will forgive me, but because you continue to teach and renew my heart in your grace. Amen.

Assurance: **God expects me to forgive others.**

Day 5

"And forgive us our debts,
as we also have forgiven our debtors."
Matthew 6:12 NRSV

Thought: A debt can be a serious burden, whether financial, physical, or emotional. A debt causes strain on your resources; it creates both internal and external pressure. The obligation of debt carries over into all aspects of life. The relief when a debt is paid or even better, forgiven, is indescribable. This is the rush of spiritual freedom at the heart of forgiveness for others.

Prayer: God, forgiveness of others is an obligation of your forgiveness. May I offer forgiveness freely to others, even as I am freely forgiven by you. Amen.

Assurance: **Indebtedness is released through forgiveness.**

Day 6

*"If you forgive others their trespasses, your heavenly
Father will also forgive you."*
Matthew 6:14 NRSV

Thought: To understand more about forgiving others, consider whom you actually need to forgive. Is there ill will in your heart toward someone you know who conveniently ducked rather than engaged with you when your loved one died? Do you cherish resentment toward a minister or clergy who was more clinical than pastoral about the death of your loved one, or perhaps who did not show up at all at your time of greatest spiritual need? Are you reluctant to forgive someone, perhaps a friend, who should have followed up, checked on you, and cared more about your grief?

Prayer: God, my laundry list of hurts is disproportionate to my desire to forgive and be forgiven. I pray for the resolve to let go and live in the grace of your forgiveness. Amen.

Assurance: **I am ready to forgive the unintentional slights of others.**

Day 7 – Rest for Your Soul

*"If you do not forgive others, neither will your
Father forgive your trespasses."*
Matthew 6:15 NRSV

Thought: Family dysfunction, separation, and estrangement may be part of the fallout of grief. Often this is caused by human, free-will choices and decisions. Despite the representations of advertising, there are no perfect families. There may be no other way to practice forgiveness except to move beyond and let go of situations and people along the rough road through grief. Forgive others from the perspective of your vision of the future.

Prayer: God, my heart is open to forgive others. On this day of rest, may my soul find its center in your divine forgiveness. Amen.

Assurance: **I repair relationships when I forgive.**

Perspective

And, above everything else, be truly loving, for love is the
golden chain of all the virtues.
Colossians 3:14 JBP

Thought: The truth about love is this: the more there is, the more there is to give away. Love grows exponentially. Love costs nothing and flourishes with its steady care and nurture. Grief teaches the immutable, everlasting nature of love. Love can outlast anything. God speaks to you continually of God's love, the one thing that stands when everything else has fallen. Finally, yours is the victory in grief when you forgive yourself and others from a heart filled with gratitude to God in Christ.

Prayer: God, the beauty of love is forever. May I live forward, restored by the grace of your life-sustaining love. Amen.

Assurance: **Love grows in love. Love grows from love.**

Grief Is Love

GRIEF IS LIFE

Leighton preached on what the Bible has to say about daily living. His message was that everyone at some time has a mountaintop experience that soon fades into the ordinary of everyday life. Leighton and I lived on the mountaintop of sustained joy for eighteen years. Each new day was a celebration of love and delight in each other.

From the top of our mountain, grief has been a long descent into the ordinariness of life. I now understand better why joy is so elusive. Over the course of Leighton's illness, a part of me—the part brimming with love and joy for Leighton, for life, and for the future—died a hard, bitter death. When he died, it seemed that my joy died, too. Life has been a lonely, uphill struggle without him at my side. How do I scale some new height when the mountain has crumbled?

At the top of Pike's Peak, a fourteen-thousand-foot elevation with a breathtaking vista that on a clear day seems like a view to all of life, I stood in reverent silence and read the plaque commemorating the poem "America the Beautiful" by Katherine Lee Bates, inspired by her 1893 visit to the mountain, about which she wrote: "All the wonder of America seemed displayed there, with the sea-like expanse."* To experience such wonder at that place on that day was a cameo moment of reawakening to life—an instant when you take a mental photograph of the scene, forever imprinting on your mind and heart the smell, taste, and warmth—that perfect oneness with all of creation that lasts forever. Thanks be to God for life, beautiful life.

*From "About El Paso County, Colorado,"
http://adm2.elpasoco.com/epchome/plaque.asp. December 19, 2011.

Preparation

Now choose life, so that you and your children may live and that you may love the LORD your God, listen to his voice, and hold fast to him.
For the LORD is your life .
Deuteronomy 30:19-20 NIV

Thought: Though grief is an inevitable part of life, no one grieves in the same way or at the same pace. Your grief is personal; it cannot be neatly confined to a set number of weeks or months. You grieve as long as you must grieve. Yet one day, someday, you find yourself unexpectedly at the end of the grief journey, wavering between the past and the future. This is the moment when you decide emphatically to choose life. You rejoin life in the fullness for which God created you. You honor the steadfast love and faithfulness of God when you resolve to live the rest of the life that is yours, empowered by your own extraordinary gifts of grief.

Prayer: God, you are my life. I love you. Through the long journey of grief I have listened to your voice and held fast to you. I give thanks that because of your unfailing grace I now am ready to live again. Amen.

Assurance: **Choose life!**

Week 1 – Contentment

Day 1

If they obey and serve him, they will spend the rest of their days in prosperity and their years in contentment.
Job 36:11 NIV

Thought: When you realize that you again feel some contentment in life, you acknowledge with gratitude and perhaps relief that the hard-fought struggle with grief is over. As you abandon the defensiveness of grief, life slowly shifts to sustained contentment. Your spirit is open again to new possibilities. You are ready to go forth and live in the spiritual prosperity of obedience and service.

Prayer: God, in grief I sense the need for obedience and service in order to at last find contentment. I pray for a calm spirit focused on your promises for life. Amen.

Assurance: **I resolve to spend the rest of my years in contentment.**

Day 2

The fear of the LORD leads to life;
then one rests content, untouched by trouble.
Proverbs 19:23 NIV

Thought: What is contentment? Contentment is an emotional achievement of grief. It is the defeat of chronic upset, fear, and anxiety. If you think about the road on your journey through the valley of the shadow of death, there have been many stops along the way. Contentment is the final plateau on the way out of grief. For a while, it is a good enough place to be.

Prayer: God, in contentment I feel less touched by the trouble of death and grief. I honor you because I know that you are leading me back to life. Amen.

Assurance: **My contentment is the prelude to my peace.**

Day 3

Be content with what you have; for he has said, "I will never
leave you or forsake you."
Hebrews 13:5 NRSV

Thought: Though you still may feel lonely or alone, at last you are growing accustomed to the physical absence of the one lost to you in death. Grief may still wash over you from time to time, yet it cannot drown you again with its pain and sorrow. The certainty of life after death and life beyond death both assures and comforts your healing heart. Your quiet contentment honors the living memory your loved one.

Prayer: God, I am content because I know that you never leave me or forsake me. Your presence sustains my faith and hope. Amen.

Assurance: **My contentment is a sure sign that I am healing.**

Day 4

Of course, there is great gain in godliness combined with contentment.
1 Timothy 6:6 NRSV

Thought: Contentment is a place of emotional neutral. It is neither the overwhelming sorrow of darkest grief nor the excitement of great hope for the future.

Contentment is a momentary resting place for your soul where you pause for refreshment after the dynamic turbulence of active grief. Contentment is learning again to exhale, even as you inhale the sweet smell of new life that awaits you.

Prayer: God, you show me godliness within contentment. I am grateful for the refreshment of my life in your spirit. Amen.

Assurance: **My grief is about gain in godliness and contentment.**

Day 5

I have learned to be content with whatever I have.
Philippians 4:11 NRSV

Thought: What you have now after the death of your loved one is not what you planned for or counted on in life. You miss the sweet and the simple moments of daily interaction. You even miss the routine, the order, and the very predictability of life. Contentment is learning to be satisfied with what is, rather than longing for what was. Contentment is part of the learning curve of grief.

Prayer: God, you encourage me in the tranquility of contentment. At this final station of grief, may I be content with today and hope for tomorrow. Amen.

Assurance: **I will be content with what I have.**

Day 6

I know what it is to be in need, and I know what it is to have plenty. I have learned the secret of being content in any and every situation, whether well fed or hungry, whether living in plenty or in want.
Philippians 4:12 NIV

Thought: There is great triumph in contentment. When you are gradually refilled with life after the physical and emotional drain of grief, you better understand the contrast between need and plenty. For a while, grief feels like a starvation diet. You hunger for love, for the presence of your loved one, and for life as it was in the past. When at last you realize that you are content, you understand that you have been nourished by grief with the real food of life.

Prayer: God, grief has within many secrets that you have graciously revealed to me over time. Thank you for the contrast of need and plenty and for your soul-satisfying grace. Amen.

Assurance: **I find contentment in plenty and in my want.**

Day 7 – Rest for Your Soul

My soul is satisfied as with a rich feast,
and my mouth praises you with joyful lips

. . . .

for you have been my help,
and in the shadow of your wings I sing for joy.
Psalm 63:5, 7 NRSV

Thought: At last you take your place again at the rich feast of life. In thanksgiving, you rejoice because grief finds no place at your table and does not intrude on the meal. You eat with spiritual abandon of the goodness of life. You are content with the menu. You enjoy and are satisfied. You sing and make music. You are alive.

Prayer: God, on this day of rest my soul is content with the feast of your love. You have been my help. May I abide forever in the shadow of your wings. Amen.

Assurance: **I am grateful to God for life.**

Week 2 – Peace

Day 1

And the peace of God, which surpasses
all understanding, will guard your hearts and
your minds in Christ Jesus.
Philippians 4:7 NRSV

Thought: Peace is deep spiritual contentment. It is the exquisite, calm silence within that simply is. Peace does not overwhelm you all at once and for all time. You are not suddenly there. Peace comes in small, elusive moments when fleeting glints of emotional sunshine warm your heart and then fade. Your moments of peace recur with greater frequency until at last your life is more about contentment than pain and more about peace than grief.

Prayer: God, your peace surpasses every human understanding of life. I pray that you will continue to guard my heart and mind in the peace of Christ. Amen.

Assurance: **Peace is beyond my understanding.**

Day 2

And let the peace of Christ rule in your hearts. . . . And be thankful.
Colossians 3:15 NRSV

Thought: For a while it seems the only thing that rules in your heart is grief. Grief takes control and reigns over your every thought and feeling. Slowly and surely it is deposed by peace. It may happen that the emotions of grief still show up from time to time to seize your contentment and peace. When the peace of Christ rules in your heart, the battle with grief is forever won.

Prayer: God, I am profoundly thankful that there is peace in my life again. Christ rules over grief in my heart. Amen.

Assurance: **Peace inspires my thankfulness.**

Day 3

Peace I leave with you; my peace I give to you. I do not give to you as the world gives. Do not let your hearts be troubled, and do not let them be afraid.
John 14:27 NRSV

Thought: Christ calmed the confusion of his disciples about his life and impending death with words of peace. He affirmed that peace is his legacy. He gave them the gift of peace. He explained that his peace is different from that of the world. His peace is eternal. Christ understood the fear and confusion of anticipatory grief. Today and every day, God assures you of the peace of Christ.

Prayer: God, in peace I experience the power and presence of Christ. I am grateful for your eternal inheritance of peace. Amen.

Assurance: **In Christ I have living peace.**

Day 4

*Let us therefore make every effort to do what leads
to peace and to mutual edification.*
Romans 14:19 NIV

Thought: You move beyond grief as you grow in your capacity for peace and mutual edification. What is mutual edification? It is the encouragement and building up of others. You give the gift of yourself when you "serve one another in love" (Galatians 5:13 NIV). A heart of service offered in peace thrives in perpetuity.

Imperceptibly you contribute to the formation of others when you serve in love and peace.

Prayer: God, you have brought me through the chaos of grief and blessed my life with peace once again. May I serve others in your name for mutual edification. Amen.

Assurance: **I pursue peace when I serve others.**

Day 5

For the kingdom of God is not food and drink but righteousness and peace and joy in the Holy Spirit.
Romans 14:17 NRSV

Thought: You are near the end of the journey through grief when you claim for yourself the gift of peace. You are at peace because you have forgiven yourself your human insufficiency to death. You are at peace because you no longer strain against what you cannot change. You are at peace because you have traveled the valley of the shadow of death and found on the other side, not food and drink, but righteousness, peace, and joy.

Prayer: God, you intimate your kingdom through the gift of peace. I give you thanks for the power and steady presence of the Holy Spirit, which is transforming my life unto peace. Amen.

Assurance: **God's estate is righteousness, peace, and joy.**

Day 6

If it is possible, so far as it depends on you, live peaceably with all.
Romans 12:18 NRSV

Thought: Inner peace is just that—yours alone. But peace is also an obligation of community. It does not thrive in the isolation of personal privacy. If you have peace, you are called to bear peace and live peaceably with others. Imagine a world in which those who know peace spread it with spiritual passion like a contagion. It is impossible to go through grief and survive it without sharing the encouragement of peace with others at the end of the journey.

Prayer: God, you ask those who receive your peace to live in peace with others. I am grateful that you have blessed me with peace once again. May I be an agent of peace in your name. Amen.

Assurance: **I will be a servant of peace in the world.**

Day 7 – Rest for Your Soul

But the fruit of the Spirit is love, joy, peace, patience, kindness, goodness, faithfulness, gentleness and self-control.
Galatians 5.22-23 NIV

Thought: The fruit of the Spirit encompasses the eternal qualities of life. Peace is found in patience. Peace is found in kindness. Peace is found in goodness. Peace is found in gentleness. Peace is found in self-control. The enduring measure of your spirit is your lifetime endowment to those you love. Plant, grow, and harvest. Be fruitful in your legacy of peace.

Prayer: God, the fruit of the Spirit is rich and abundant. Your fruit is eternal. On this day of rest my soul is at peace with you. Amen.

Assurance: **Peace is fruit of my spirit.**

Week 3 – Happiness

Day 1

Happy are those who make
*the L*ORD *their trust.*
Psalm 40:4 NRSV

Thought: As your grief moves into new, unexplored spiritual and emotional territory, you may ask yourself, "Will I ever be happy again?" Your answer is perhaps, "I might be happy again if only something would change so that everything would be better." This conclusion denies the reality of where you have been and where you are going as you take your leave of grief. Be assured that you will be happy again.

Prayer: God, I want to be happy again. I am grateful that this is possible when I make you my trust. Amen.

Assurance: **God is my trust.**

Day 2

Happy are those whose strength is in you.
Psalm 84:5 NRSV

Thought: What is happiness? The root *hap*, meaning "luck, chance, or good for-tune," is found in words of both positive and negative connotation: happening, mishap, haphazard, happenstance.* The implied meaning of happiness is that luck, chance, and good fortune determine your state of being. This suggests that you are not entirely in charge of your own happiness. The truth is that there is nothing random about happiness. It is a choice you can make for the rest of your life.

Prayer: God, my strength is in you. You have supported and sustained me through grief in the way that leads to happiness in you. Amen.

Assurance: **God's strength ordains my happiness.**

Day 3

Happy are those whom you discipline, O Lord.
Psalm 94:12 NRSV

Thought: For some, happiness is a way of life. Those with a naturally sunny dis-position are often sustained through grief by a greater sense of hope and optimism than those who are by nature more introverted or reserved. In grief, happiness comes to you indirectly. It is the result of something you have already done: you have grieved. Happiness, then, is a reward at the end of the journey through grief.

Prayer: God, you have gently yet firmly disciplined me to do the work of grief. I am grateful for your direction and guidance in the way toward happiness in you. Amen.

Assurance: **God's discipline instructs my happiness.**

Day 4

Happy are those who find wisdom,
and those who get understanding.
Proverbs 3:13 NRSV

Thought: Happiness is the by-product of your inner stability rather than your out-ward security. When you grieve, you explore and discover, perhaps for the first time in life, the depth of your inner stability. Although your sense of well-being is affected by death, you are not wholly at the mercy of happenstance or outward circumstance. Rather, happiness is the triumph of your inner stability over your outward security.

American Heritage® Dictionary of the English Language, 4th ed., s.v. "hap."

Prayer: God, spiritual understanding is the wisdom of grief. I am grateful for a new perspective of happiness for the rest of my life. Amen.

Assurance: **Grief teaches me both understanding and wisdom.**

Day 5

And now, my children, listen to me:
happy are those who keep my ways.
Proverbs 8:32 NRSV

Thought: In grief, quiet desperation, loneliness, and emotional misery often drive the pursuit of superficial happiness. The media suggest every day what will make you happy. Family and friends want to reconstruct your happiness according to their idea of your well-being. Happiness begins where you are. It happens within your heart.

Prayer: God, as your child I listen to hear your voice. May I keep your ways in faithfulness to your will. Amen.

Assurance: **Happiness is an inside story.**

Day 6

You shall eat the fruit of the labour of your hands; you
shall be happy, and it shall go well with you.
Psalm 128:2 NRSV

Thought: As life unfolds beyond the broken heart, happiness is not an instantaneous state of undiluted pleasure. Slowly, your renewed energy begins to feel like happiness as life fills you again with the seeping warmth of hope. If what you experience is not exactly happiness, then perhaps it is peace merely waiting to grow and flourish.

Prayer: God, grief is a labor of love that bears fruit in happiness. I am grateful that life is better in the promise of your grace. Amen.

Assurance: **The orchard of grief bears happiness for me.**

Day 7 – Rest for Your Soul

Happy are the people whose God is the LORD.
Psalm 144:15 NRSV

Thought: A life of service is the secret to happiness. The happy person reaches out to comfort, having been comforted. The happy person loves, having been loved. The happy person finds new life by giving it away. It is true that in giving you receive and in selflessness you find. This is the authentic happiness of a life well lived. Spiritual happiness is only a small step away from joy— the ultimate quest of your journey through grief.

Prayer: God, you have directed my path on the journey through grief. On this day of rest my soul finds happiness in you. Amen.

Assurance: **I will live in the sustained happiness of God.**

Week 4 – Joy

Day 1

This is the day that the LORD has made;
let us rejoice and be glad in it.
Psalm 118:24 NRSV

Thought: Joy is the perfect balance of peace and hope at the depth of your inmost soul. In joy you are at one with God and with yourself, whatever the circumstances of life may be. In joy the noise of insistent grief is at last silent. Joy is spiritual delight. Joy is the beauty of a roseate sunset. In joy colors seem particularly acute. Joy is filtered sunlight through the majesty of trees. In joy light is the beacon of life.

Prayer: God, you are the Creator. Each new day is a gift of life. In joy I am again glad to be alive. I look for you in all creation. Amen.

Assurance: **Joy is oneness with the moment of life that is this very day.**

Day 2

Be glad in the LORD and rejoice, O righteous,
and shout for joy, all you upright in heart.
Psalm 32:11 NRSV

Thought: When you near the end of grief, you realize perhaps that you have neglected joy along the journey. Think about what joy really is, especially from the perspective of your experience of grief. It looks and feels different now, doesn't it? You may need to devote spiritual energy to the awareness that is necessary to relearn joy. In grief this is re-joicing, remembering the glory of joy and making joy a habit. Consider joy, practice joy, look for joy.

Prayer: God, I recall the deep spiritual satisfaction of joy. I pray that I may at last shout again for joy. Amen.

Assurance: **Soul joy is an active pursuit.**

Day 3

"Until now you have not asked for anything in my name. Ask and you will receive, so that your joy may be complete."
John 16:24 NRSV

Thought: As grief gradually wanes and then fades, you perhaps focus on the questions of life beyond your broken heart. How do you connect and serve again in joy? What is the life force, the motivation, or the impetus of your daily existence? Is it momentary pleasure or life-satisfying joy? Why is it so difficult to relax and enjoy life? Will the cloud of grief overshadow your life forever? Will God ever surprise you again in life with joy? Where do you find fullness of joy? What is complete joy?

Prayer: God, I come to you with the questions of new life. I am grateful for life unfolding in the joy of your grace. Amen.

Assurance: **When I ask, I believe that I receive.**

Day 4

"Now is your time of grief, but I will see you again and you will rejoice, and no one will take away your joy."
John 16:22 NIV

Thought: At last grief turns to joy when life blossoms in unexpected ways that bring hope for the future. Grief turns to joy with the birth of a child or grandchild. Grief turns to joy in moments that celebrate love. Grief turns to joy with a new partner for the rest of life's journey. And finally, grief turns to joy when at last we are reunited with the one we have grieved in life and in death. From grief comes joy.

Prayer: God, you have led me through grief toward the hope of new life. I rejoice in the promise of eternal reunion in you. Amen.

Assurance: **Joy cannot be taken away from me.**

Day 5

You have turned my mourning into dancing;
you have taken off my sackcloth and clothed me with joy,
so that my soul may praise you and not be silent.
O LORD my God, I will give thanks to you forever.
Psalm 30:11-12 NRSV

Thought: Grief turns into dancing when your zest for new life simply can no longer be contained. You want to live again in exuberant joy. On that day you cast aside forever the symbolic garments of grief, ready to put on the fresh new suit of joy. Joy is the moment when it is impossible to be silent or wait even one minute longer for new life to burst forth. Your soul at last rejoices.

Prayer: God, joy is refreshment for my soul after the long journey through grief. I can no longer be silent. I give thanks to you forever. Amen.

Assurance: **At last I dance for joy.**

Day 6

Rejoice in the Lord always; again I will say, Rejoice.
Philippians 4:4 NRSV

Thought: Joy is the enrichment of love. Joy is the uplift of peace. Joy is the benefit of trust. Joy is the radiance of hope. Joy is the light of faith. Though you can't touch it or feel it or smell it or hold it, joy is the substance of your soul. Reawaken to life in the glory of joy.

Prayer: God, I rejoice in you always. May I be as faithful to you in joy as you have been to me in grief. Amen.

Assurance: **I rejoice—again and again and again.**

Day 7 – Rest for Your Soul

This day is holy to our LORD; and do not be grieved, for the joy
of the LORD is your strength.
Nehemiah 8:10 NRSV

Thought: In grief, sadness may become a comfortable habit. With your loved one, there was great joy. Grief teaches you that it is not a betrayal of the one lost to you in death to be joyful again in life. Joy may require both practice and discipline of the spirit. Resolving the issue of joy is a finishing touch to grief. Take up your life where it is. Move on and beyond in fullness of joy.

Prayer: God, on this day of rest may I abide in your holiness. I am grateful for the joy of your strength in my soul. Amen.

Assurance: **In joy there is strength for my new life.**

Perspective

You show me the path of life.
In your presence there is fullness of joy;
in your right hand are pleasures for evermore.
Psalm 16:11 NRSV

Thought: When your journey through grief is at an end, it is your sacred duty to choose life. Contentment intimates that there is life beyond grief. Peace assures you that life will again be good and whole. Happiness suggests that your soul yet again will be flooded with joy. In joy you live again in rich fullness, restored to beauty, possibility, and wonder. Choose life. Flourish and serve.

Prayer: God, you show me the path of life. I am grateful that there is fullness of joy in your presence. Amen.

Assurance: **God wants me to live. God needs me to live. God wants me to *want* to live.**

Grief Is Life

_____

_____

_____

_____

_____

_____

_____

_____

_____

_____

_____

_____

_____

_____

_____

_____

GRIEF IS CELEBRATION

Even though I grieved, I knew I must not block the festivities of the holiday season entirely from my life. I was allowed to participate. And so I allowed my pragmatic resistance to all things commercial to thaw a bit. I mixed it up with the crowds to see what it was all about. I listened to the high energy of noise all around and watched for sights that awakened my spirit as I tentatively moved again toward Emmanuel.

On the sidewalk a solo trombonist played with off-key abandon, "O Come, O Come, Emmanuel." His music drew me in as I sensed my heart awakening to its message. As I waited for a cab, I heard a street-corner rendition of "Angels We Have Heard on High." Suddenly I remembered that this is my favorite Christmas carol and felt a small smile of joy within. The lights on Park Avenue shouted, "It's not too late; don't miss it!" There was urgency in their message of joy. At church the sermon on awakening seeped through my spiritual consciousness. The smell of incense assaulted my senses with its mysterious, curling smoke, the symbol of prayer and hope.

I was humbled by the man on the street who had only one foot. He silently asked for alms, his dignity fully intact. He seemed genuinely surprised and grateful when I at once honored his wordless entreaty and affirmed his human need. His dog was with him, perhaps to give him warmth. Or perhaps he helped his master as the faithful companion that he was. The man had a friend; on that day he was less alone than I was.

The man who slept most every night wedged into a side doorway at the church was not in his usual place. Yet his neatly packed worldly possessions stood on the sidewalk in testimony to his very existence. I tucked a bill into his bundle. It was my Christmas joy to provide even a small token in acknowledgment of his life. Perhaps when he unrolled his bed in search of warmth and protection from another freezing night he found the gift and knew that someone cared. Emmanuel, God with us. I am on the way to the manger to celebrate Christ.

Preparation

I will be with you; I will not fail you or forsake you.
Joshua 1:5 NRSV

Thought: Grief is an experience that often collides with the ongoing celebrations of life. Your journey through grief is marked by inevitable secular and sacred holidays. If daily life with your loved one was a continuous festival of love and joy, you may grieve the loss of celebration in your life. Even under the best circumstances, holidays are emotion-laden occasions. When you grieve at the holidays, you agonize about what is to come because of the unknown—that is, how things will be rather than how things have been. Likely you live in the shadow of expectation; you cherish high hopes and dismal fears. Most often reality is somewhere in between.

Prayer: God, I am anxious about the holiday season and how it will be without my loved one. May I rest in the assurance that you will hold me close as I grieve and remember. Amen.

Assurance: **God is with me.**

Week 1 – Holidays

Day 1

Be strong and of good courage, do not fear or be in dread . . . for it is the LORD your God who goes with you; he will not fail you or forsake you.
Deuteronomy 31:6 RSV

Thought: You may be among the many people who dread the holidays because of the unavoidable pressure to do, buy, and experience all that is urged upon you during the season. The nature of grief is that it intensifies your experience of occasions that painfully remind you of your loss. Fear and dread may creep into your heart as you begin to imagine what the holiday season will be like. You may ask, "How can there be celebration without the one I love?"

Prayer: God, I know that you go with me into the uncharted territory of holiday celebration without my loved one. I pray that you will quiet the fear and dread of grief that threaten my heart. Amen.

Assurance: **There will be other holidays.**

Day 2

Have no dread of them, for the LORD your God, who is present with you, is a great and awesome God.
Deuteronomy 7:21 NRSV

Thought: When you grieve, it is normal to entertain a certain dread of the holiday season. Dread is disquiet within your heart. Dread is worry. Dread may show up as emotional or physical distress. Dread is often just the simple human misery of loneliness. In the extreme, dread is fear, a very human response to grief. As you approach the holiday season, remember that anticipation is usually much worse than the actual holiday. Often you resolve much of your fear ahead of time, and the day is not as difficult as you expect.

Prayer: God, I am awash in dread, fearful of the holiday season ahead. I give thanks that you are a great and awesome God. Amen.

Assurance: **I will think about making it through just this holiday.**

Day 3

*May those who sow in tears
reap with shouts of joy.*
Psalm 126:5 NRSV

Thought: If this is the first holiday season without your loved one, you may be engulfed by a tidal wave of emotion. When you grieve at the holidays, your heart is particularly attuned to the sadness of loss and pain. If you are tearful or depressed, your heartfelt tears may cue your family members to express their emotions as well. Worry about crying is a hardship of grief compounded by the holidays. When you release your tears, you experience physical and emotional relief, a welcome catharsis to your grief.

Prayer: God, it is difficult to imagine that one day the tears of grief for my loved one will turn to joy. I pray for the reassurance of your presence at this emotional time of the year. Amen.

Assurance: **I resolve to guard my heart because the holidays are the most stressful time of the year.**

Day 4

"But the cares of the world and the lure of wealth choke the word."
Matthew 13:22 NRSV

Thought: Likely you know the instinctive sense of aversion when print advertising and television commercials assault you prematurely with stealth campaigns that inevitably draw your attention to the extended holiday season. It seems that advertising and decorating begin earlier each year. You are inescapably hostage to rampant commercialism. Inwardly you perhaps groan, but at some point likely you succumb to its banal urgency. Manage the artificial insistence of the commercial holiday season one day at a time.

Prayer: God, the cares of my own small world seem enlarged by the holiday season. I pray for strength and resolve to resist the world and live in your Word. Amen.

Assurance: **I will set realistic expectations for myself and for the holiday.**

Day 5

"Give us this day our daily bread."
Matthew 6:11 NRSV

Thought: The actual holiday is just one day, twenty-four hours. For weeks on end, life is pressured by commercial, social, and spiritual suggestions that demand a larger-than-life experience of the holiday. Inflamed by the secular world, intense emotions overlay grief for what seems an interminable holiday season. The holiday itself is just one day. Put the day in perspective. Live only in this day.

Prayer: God, you do not ask me to live more than one day at a time. I am grateful for your daily provision for my life and soul. Amen.

Assurance: **I will stay in the moment that is today.**

Day 6

*You remember me in everything and maintain the traditions
just as I handed them on to you.*
1 Corinthians 11:2 NRSV

Thought: Holidays usually center on tradition. As the season approaches, your family may want everything "back to normal." You may feel subtle pressure to be appropriately cheerful and gay. Your family may expect you to "be over" your grief. With the death of your loved one, family traditions may continue, or new traditions that honor his or her memory may be created. What you do this year does not have to become a permanent tradition. Your experience of grief may change the way you approach the holiday season. You may decide on a new format for the future.

Prayer: God, your Word teaches the sanctity of spiritual tradition. May your grace be the unchanging tradition in my soul at this holiday season and always. Amen.

Assurance: **I resolve to have a "good enough" holiday, rather than a perfect holiday.**

Day 7 – Rest for Your Soul

Rest in the Lord and wait patiently for him.
Psalm 37:7 KJV

Thought: Take time for yourself on holidays—time to reflect, time to remember, time to forget. Let others know that they are not responsible for making you happy. Even if your loved one would want you to be happy, you do not have to be happy. Being happy, however, does not deny your grief for your loved one. When one day life returns more to happiness, holidays will be easier to manage. The experience of most people who are grieving is that eventually they do enjoy the holidays again.

Prayer: God, I would like to speed through rather than wait patiently for your lessons of grief at the holidays. On this day of rest may my soul wait for you. Amen.

Assurance: **I will remember to rest; the holidays are emotionally and physically draining.**

Week 2 – Festival

Day 1

But the angel said to them, "Do not be afraid; for see—I am bringing you good news of great joy for all the people."
Luke 2:10 NRSV

Thought: Christmas may evoke memories that trigger or sustain your grief. The contrast between sorrow and celebration is almost unbearable because many of your best memories are perhaps in the context of holiday celebrations. You may be painfully aware of the absence of your loved one, who likely was among the most important people in your interpersonal sphere. You endow Christmas with emotional power as you remember the past with intense yearning for the one whose presence brought such joy to your life.

Prayer: God, you calm my fears through the voice of those who speak to me of comfort at Christmas. I am grateful for the good news of great joy that overcomes death and grief. Amen.

Assurance: **God knows my heart as I grieve at Christmas.**

Day 2

Therefore the Lord himself will give you a sign. Look, the young woman is with child and shall bear a son, and shall name him Emmanuel.
Isaiah 7:14 NRSV

Thought: The festival of Christmas celebrates the season and the day. Likely your secular reference is tradition, now changed by the loss of your loved one. Is it too much effort to put up a tree? Do you decorate, or should the ornaments stay packed away this year? Is it too painful for you to send Christmas cards? Is gift selection a daunting task without your loved one? As you gather with family, or others you choose as family, you realize that the festival of Christmas will never be the same again without your loved one.

Prayer: God, the birth of Christ is the miracle to celebrate at this Christmas season. I am grateful that through this holy gift of your love you are with me. Amen.

Assurance: **Emmanuel—God with us.**

Day 3

This will be a sign for you: you will find a child wrapped in
bands of cloth and lying in a manger.
Luke 2:12 NRSV

Thought: Within the festival your heart seeks the deeper experience of Christmas, a personal encounter with the child in the manger. Sometimes it happens; sometimes it does not. For a while, your joy in the world may seem a remembrance from a life passed away. But Christmas is about new life. In the birth of a perfect child, the vitality of soul and spirit is wrapped in love and hope for the future.

Prayer: God, you came to earth in the perfection of Christ to show us your love. I kneel at the manger in thanks and adoration. Amen.

Assurance: **Christmas is wrapped in a child.**

Day 4

And suddenly there was with the angel a multitude of the
heavenly host, praising God and saying,
"Glory to God in the highest heaven, and on earth
peace among those whom he favours!"
Luke 2:13-14 NRSV

Thought: Christmas may come to you in small, private moments when your heart is strangely touched by joy. The experience of Christmas may surprise you with the mystery of its comfort. Amid the chaos of grief, the moment of Christmas may take your breath away with its life-renewing peace. Look for a sign; it will overwhelm you as the certainty of life beyond death reaches into your heart with the unmistakable gift of God's love.

Prayer: God, I join with the angels in singing your praise. I am grateful for your peace on earth and in my heart. Amen.

Assurance: **God favors me with heavenly love.**

Day 5

When the angels had left them and gone into heaven, the shepherds said to one
another, "Let us go now to Bethlehem and see this thing that has taken place,
which the Lord has made known to us."
Luke 2:15 NRSV

Thought: When the angels appeared to the shepherds, they were at first incredulous and then overcome with fear. After the moment of announcement, awe, and wonder, they talked it over and decided to go see what it all meant. They knew with simple certainty that God was the bearer of this extraordinary good news. They did not know what to expect, but they were willing to make the effort to get to the manger. This is the journey of grief at Christmas.

Prayer: God, the shepherds entertained angels and received the good news. I pray for the spiritual energy to make my way to the manger to worship Christ the child. Amen.

Assurance: **I will go to the manger for the experience of Christmas.**

Day 6

So they went with haste and found Mary and Joseph,
and the child lying in the manger.
Luke 2:16 NRSV

Thought: Grief is an opportunity to discover anew the true meaning of Christmas—God's love for humankind. Christmas happens when you discern God's divine love in your heart. This is the love that holds you close in grief. This is the love that restores you and makes you whole again. Emmanuel—God with you to comfort you, to redeem you, to give you peace.

Prayer: God, my heart is open to what I will find at the manger. May I hurry toward Christmas to discover again the rich gift of your love. Amen.

Assurance: **I celebrate new life from grief.**

Day 7 – Rest for Your Soul

The shepherds returned, glorifying and praising God for all they
had heard and seen, as it had been told them.
Luke 2:20 NRSV

Thought: The experience of Christmas may come to you any day, not just December 25. Expect it. Be open to it. Christmas comes when someone reaches out to you in love. Christmas comes when you reach out to someone in love. Expect an unexpected blessing. Be a blessing to others. Christmas. Emmanuel. God with us. God with you.

Prayer: God, on this day of rest for my soul I marvel anew at all that you do in love for me. Amen.

Assurance: **Christmas is the miracle of love.**

Week 3 – Experience

Day 1

*The sun shall no longer be
your light by day,
nor for brightness shall the moon
give light to you by night;
but the LORD will be your everlasting light,
and your God will be your glory.*
Isaiah 60:19 NRSV

Thought: Christmas lights symbolize the festival. Each one is a brilliant celebration of life. The reality of grief is that the death of your loved one has darkened your life. At Christmas, darkness seeks the light and becomes the light. The light of promise that there is yet life beyond grief shines within your darkness. Christmas is about the light of the world, God's love illuminating your darkness.

Prayer: God, you are everlasting light. At this Christmas season, may I actively seek your light within the darkness of my grief. Amen.

Assurance: **I will live in the bright glory of God's eternal light.**

Day 2

*Light dawns for the righteous,
and joy for the upright in heart.*
Psalm 97:11 NRSV

Thought: There are many incarnations of light—candlelight, incandescent light, sunlight, moonlight, the radiance of brilliant stars. In grief, light is the delicate balance between sadness and your hope for the future. Light is your enjoyment of one or two aspects of the holiday season and your ability to survive largely intact. Light is your heightened peace. Light is your understanding of the gift of joy.

Prayer: God, you give light and joy in Christ. May I honor your gift with an upright heart that refuses to be forever darkened by grief. Amen.

Assurance: **In light I see the dawn of new life.**

Day 3

But the path of the righteous is like the light of dawn,
which shines brighter and brighter until full day.
Proverbs 4:18 NRSV

Thought: Just as there is no one experience of loss, so there is no one experience of light. Light shines in quiet meditation. Light shines in moments of prayer and thanksgiving. Light shines when you light a candle to honor the memory of your loved one. Remember that your shared light shines forever. Love is the divine link to the eternal spiritual presence of the one you have loved and lost. As you create light and discover your light within, each day holds the promise of remembrance, release, and expression.

Prayer: God, the light of Christmas dawns in my heart. I pray that it will shine brighter and brighter until I live again in the full light of your grace. Amen.

Assurance: **The light of love shines brightly forever within me.**

Day 4

The people who walked in darkness
have seen a great light;
those who lived in a land of deep darkness—
on them light has shined.
Isaiah 9:2 NRSV

Thought: The invisible framework of a tunnel is an apt metaphor for God's unseen presence at work in your life. In grief, God is the foundation that holds and supports you. There are obstacles and stops along the way through the darkness of grief, yet you trust God, the infrastructure, to keep you safe. As you emerge again from the dark place that is grief, light slowly bathes the end of the tunnel in the golden warmth of hope.

Prayer: God, you have led my walk through the land of deep darkness. I am grateful for the steady beacon of your light in Christ. Amen.

Assurance: **A great light shines on my darkness.**

Day 5

If then the light in you is darkness, how great is the darkness!
Matthew 6:23 NRSV

Thought: You have the power to direct your grief as you direct the light. Whether your grief is still profound heartache or now more about acceptance than pain, a dark corner of the heart forever quietly swirls with questions of life and death. Finding the light means managing the darkness. Unlike gradations of light, dark is dark. In darkness there is only darkness. When you block the light and instead choose darkness, you become a holiday victim. Seek the light.

Prayer: God, in grief I live more in darkness than in light. In this Christmas season I pray that you will illuminate the darkness of my heart and spirit with your light. Amen.

Assurance: **In darkness there is no light.**

Day 6

If I say, "Surely the darkness shall cover me,
and the light around me become night,"
even the darkness is not dark to you;
the night is as bright as the day
for darkness is as light to you.
Psalm 139:11-12 NRSV

Thought: At Christmas, chaos may roil your emotions. There may be chaos in your family or home. The clamor of the secular world may incite chaos in your heart. But chaos is overwhelmed and defeated by light. The light of God's love is the reason for Christmas. As you slowly order the chaos of grief, darkness is overcome by the light of renewed life. It is the light of God's eternal love that guides your way through the darkness of grief.

Prayer: God, in the gift of Christ, fear and chaos lose their say in life. I pray that the night of my grief will become as bright as the day. Amen.

Assurance: **At Christmas, darkness is as light to me.**

Day 7 – Rest for Your Soul

For you have delivered my soul from death,
and my feet from falling,
so that I may walk before God
in the light of life.
Psalm 56:13 NRSV

Thought: In grief your light is overcome for a while by darkness. Then slowly and with divine radiance, the rosy aura of sunrise bathes the softness of morning with the light of reawakening life. Your journey through grief is finally illuminated by the full sunlight of joy. You have traversed the valley of the shadow of death and live again in the light of God's love. Christmas is the celebration of light. Receive the blessing when moments of light shine in your heart. Be at peace in the certainty that death is not the end.

Prayer: God, on this day of rest I know that, in Christ, my loved one lives in your light. I am grateful that you have delivered my soul from death. Amen.

Assurance: **I walk toward the light of life.**

Week 4 – Occasions

Remembrance Day

If we live, we live to the Lord, and if we die, we die to the Lord; so then,
whether we live or whether we die, we are the Lord's.
Romans 14:8 NRSV

Thought: The day on which your loved one died is a date forever etched in your heart. The first year you observe this day of days—and perhaps others yet to come—may be tearful and sorrowful. Perhaps you struggle still with guilt or regret. As days turn into weeks and weeks into months, the year goes by and life goes on. But you never forget. Sadness one day turns into grateful, warm memories of the one lost to you in death.

Prayer: God, you assure me that, in Christ, my loved one yet lives. I give you thanks for the promise of eternal life and pray that you will comfort me yet again on this remembrance day. Amen.

Assurance: **There is life after death.**

Anniversary

Let marriage be held in honour by all.
Hebrews 13:4 NRSV

Thought: Your wedding anniversary is likely an occasion that evokes memories of romance, new love, and the expectancy of a joy-filled life together. You spent part of your adult life in the relationship of marriage. You were part of a couple now physically dissolved by the event of death. Your spouse was perhaps the principal relationship of your adult life. Grief turns to joy in moments that celebrate the honor of a marriage in love and eternal commitment.

Prayer: God, you ordained the love of our marriage and sanctified our everlasting bond. I remember today with a grateful heart the love of my life here on earth. Amen.

Assurance: **I will bless others with the love of my marriage.**

Birthday

In fulfilment of his own purpose he gave us birth by the word of truth, so that we would become a kind of first fruits of his creatures.
James 1:18 NRSV

Thought: God is the giver of all life. Each person is a unique, individual creation. There are no human clones or duplicate genetic copies. No one is exactly alike. As you remember the life of your beloved on this special day, celebrate the lasting personal and spiritual legacy of the one you grieve, the one who was like no other.

Prayer: God, by the word of truth you give life to your children. I give you thanks for my loved one, a first fruit of your creation. Amen.

Assurance: **There is a purpose for every life born.**

Valentine's Day

For love is strong as death,
passion fierce as the grave.
Song of Solomon 8:6 NRSV

Thought: February 14 is largely a commercial occasion that celebrates the secular ideals of both romantic and platonic love. The love you have known with the one who has left this earth will never die. Death has separated you only in body but not in heart. As you begin to live fully beyond your grief, you acknowledge with gratitude that the grace of God is the very essence of love at work in your life.

Prayer: God, I grieve today the absence of the one lost to me in death. I celebrate the love we shared together and know that our love lives on forever. Amen.

Assurance: **Love is eternal.**

Mother's Day

> *Strength and dignity are her clothing,*
> *and she laughs at the time to come.*
> *She opens her mouth with wisdom,*
> *and the teaching of kindness is on her tongue.*
> *She looks well to the ways of her household,*
> *and does not eat the bread of idleness.*
> *Her children rise up and call her happy;*
> *her husband too, and he praises her:*
> *Many women have done excellently,*
> *but you surpass them all."*
> *Charm is deceitful, and beauty is vain,*
> *but a woman who fears the LORD is to be praised.*
> Proverbs 31:25-30 NRSV

Thought: There is perhaps no higher calling in life than to be a mother. Although many women have children, not all are mothers. You are indeed blessed if you celebrate today the life of a devoted, caring mother, a woman dedicated to the creation of a home filled with love and warmth for the nurture of family. Cherish the memory of the one who gave you life whose light shines in and through you. Give the gift of love, the legacy of your mother to future generations.

Prayer: God, you have given me life through the womanhood of a mother. Today I remember with gratitude the one who blessed me with her nurture. Amen.

Assurance: **A loving mother imprints life forever.**

Father's Day

> *Listen, children, to a father's instruction,*
> *and be attentive, that you may gain insight.*
> Proverbs 4:1 NRSV

Thought: A man fully invested in being a father understands the sacred trust of life. A father models the unconditional love of God for his children, ensuring their spiritual inheritance for generations to come. A man who cherishes his children instructs them with insight. On this special day you honor the life of the man who formed and shaped you in the eternal wisdom of God.

Prayer: God, I listen for your instruction. As I remember today the man who was my father, I give thanks for his wisdom and love. Amen.

Assurance: **The insight of a father is a glimpse into his soul.**

Memorial/Veterans Day

Therefore take up the whole armour of God, so that you may be able to withstand on that evil day, and having done everything, to stand firm. Stand therefore, and fasten the belt of truth around your waist, and put on the breastplate of righteousness. As shoes for your feet put on whatever will make you ready to proclaim the gospel of peace. With all of these, take the shield of faith, with which you will be able to quench all the flaming arrows of the evil one. Take the helmet of salvation, and the sword of the Spirit, which is the word of God.
Ephesians 6:13-17 NRSV

Thought: God is unfailing in presence to all who now serve their country. God has comforted those who throughout the ages have grieved the fallen. God honors those who make the supreme sacrifice of life to a higher cause than personal gain. God equips those whom you honor today with the spiritual endowments of one who serves—endurance, truth, faith. Remember and cherish your loved one in patriotic righteousness.

Prayer: God, I am grateful for the heroic sacrifice of all who have ever defended liberty and freedom. I remember today in reverent appreciation the life and selfless service of my loved one. Amen.

Assurance: **There is no greater love than to sacrifice it for another.**

Easter

"I am the resurrection and the life. Those who believe in me, even though they die, will live, and everyone who lives and believes in me will never die."
John 11:25-26 NRSV

Thought: Easter proclaims God's triumph over death in the resurrection of Christ from the grave. Easter proclaims God's love for you. Easter proclaims the promise of everlasting life. Because Christ lives, you live. Because Christ lives, those who believe live on after death. Easter is your faith for today and your hope for tomorrow. Easter is the victory that overcomes grief. "Why do you look for the living among the dead? He is not here, but has risen" (Luke 24:5 NRSV).

Prayer: God, in you is resurrection and life. The message of Easter assures me that my loved one is not dead but lives eternally with you. Thank you for the victory over death in Christ. Amen.

Assurance: **Rejoice in the triumph of life over death.**

All Saints' Day

Pray in the Spirit at all times in every prayer and supplication. To that end keep alert and always persevere in supplication for all the saints.
Ephesians 6:18 NRSV

Thought: Many who grieve find comfort in praying for their loved one as an act of communion. All Saints' Day commemorates the spiritual certainty that those who believe live on, perfected in heaven. Some denominations speak of believers as saints, whether living or dead. The Apostles' Creed declares, "We believe in the communion of saints." We pray for and with living saints in this life; we pray as well for and with those saints after mortal life has ceased. On this day observe the communion of saints in the fellowship of the one lost to you in death.

Prayer: God, I pray today that my loved one is at perfect peace in the joy of eternal life. Thank you that there is life beyond death as saints in your kingdom forever. Amen.

Assurance: **I pray today for all the saints, both here and in heaven.**

Thanksgiving Day

O give thanks to the LORD, for he is good;
for his steadfast love endures forever.
Psalm 107:1 NRSV

Thought: Thanksgiving Day is an all-inclusive holiday of gratitude to God for the rich heritage of a prosperous nation. This holiday is especially steeped in tradition. Without your loved one, the picture around the table is not the same as in years past. Many illustrations, such as those by Norman Rockwell, idealize the family as a multigenerational group, clearly connected by warmth and love. On this day of thanks and celebration, pass on traditions to those gathered together. Share in the love of the one departed yet dearly remembered.

Prayer: God, your goodness and steadfast love are the rich harvest of life. I celebrate today the life of the one absent from our table in thanksgiving for abundant love. Amen.

Assurance: **I give thanks for spiritual bounty**.

Christmas

"To you is born this day in the city of David a Saviour,
who is the Messiah, the Lord."
Luke 2:11 NRSV

Thought: Christmas is joy to the world. Christmas is joy in the world. Christmas is joy for the world. On this day the world rejoices that Christ is born. In fullness of joy remember the one lost to you in death. Share the gift of God's love with others. There is celebration on high; hear the angels sing.

Prayer: God, you sent Christ into a broken world to show your infinite love. My heart honors your gift of love this day and always. Amen.

Assurance: **Christmas is Christ the Lord.**

New Year's Day

By the tender mercy of our God,
the dawn from on high will break upon us,
to give light to those who sit in darkness and in the shadow of death,
to guide our feet into the way of peace.
Luke 1:78-79 NRSV

Thought: Surviving the holidays largely intact is an emotional and spiritual victory. As the new year approaches, look forward. Move toward the reality of life without your loved one. You honor the steadfast love and faithfulness of God with resolute trust in God's plan for your future. As you begin the new year, dare to contemplate the endless possibilities of life beyond death and life beyond grief. Greet the new year with hope, for with the dawn comes light and peace.

Prayer: God, as the new year approaches, I pray for renewal and personal transformation. Your tender mercy has brought light into my darkness. I am grateful that you guide my feet into the way of peace. Amen.

Assurance: **I resolve to grow toward God into the new year.**

Perspective

For with you is the fountain of life;
in your light we see light.
Psalm 36:9 NRSV

Thought: Amid the celebrations of life, there is room to grieve and grow. Beyond understanding how to manage your grief at the holiday season, you realize that there is a difference between the festival of Christmas and the experience of Christmas. As you grieve at the holidays, search for the light of Christmas shining into the depth of your soul.

Prayer: God, you are the fountain of all life. It is your light that shines into my soul through grief. I am grateful that light fills me anew with life. Amen.

Assurance: **Light and life are the celebrations of my grief.**

Grief Is Celebration